Arctic Circle

PACIFIC
OCEAN

Tropic of Cancer

Equator

INDIAN
OCEAN

Tropic of Capricorn

SOUTHERN OCEAN

Antarctic Circle

Junior
Animal
Atlas

picthall and gunzi

an imprint of Award Publications Limited

ISBN 978-1-909763-39-5

First published 2016

Written and edited by: Nina Filipek
Designed by: Jeannette O'Toole
Maps supplied by: Encompass Graphics Ltd

Images: Shutterstock. **Cover:** *Bengal tiger* – Eric Isselee, *Killer whale* – Mike Price, *Kangaroo* – Anan Kaewkhammul. **Page 1:** *Monarch butterfly* – BOONCHUAY PROMJIAM. **Page 4–5:** *Background* – Iakov Kalinin, *Fennec fox* – Robert Eastman, *Arctic fox* – Tony Campbell, *Birds on rocks* – francesco de marco, *Fish* – mexrix, *Frog* – Anneka, *Crab* – indigolotos, *Snail* – Isti2, *Monkey* – Eric Isselee, *Crocodile* – Andrew Burgess, *Octopus* – Rich Carey, *Bird* – Victor Tyakht, *Dragonfly* – Subbotina Anna, *Spider* – Aleksey Stemmer. **Page 6–7:** *Skeleton* – Potapov Alexander, *Worm* – Valentina Razumova, *Rabbit* – Kuttelvaserova Stuchelova, *Cheetah and boar* – Dennis W. Donohue, *Robin* – Daniel Zuppinger, *Plant* – netsuthep, *Caterpillar* – rotem shamli, *Blue tit* – Eric Isselee, *Hawk* – Erni, *Bee on flower* – paula french, *Squirrel* – Micky Zappa, *Polar bear* – jolly_photo, *Tamarin* – EBFoto, *Leopard* – Fulcanelli, *Children* – auremar, *Panda* – Hung Chung Chih. **Page 8–9:** *Arctic fox* – Tony Campbell, *Arctic hare* – bikeriderlondon, *Arctic tern* – Menno Schaefer, *Polar bear* – Tom linster, *Beluga whale* – Miles Away Photography, *Killer whale* – Xavier MARCHANT, *Lion's mane jellyfish* – Boris Pamikov, *Walrus* – Vladimir Melnik, *Arctic landscape* – Dmitry Kulagin. **Page 10–11:** *Wolf* – jukurae, *Wild boar* – Eric Isselee, *Young wild boar* – Eric Isselee , *Forest* – Protasov AN, *Chamois* – Incredible Arctic, *Cow* – Eric Isselee, *Dolphin* – Tory Kallman, *Camargue horses* – Jeanne Provost, *Lambs* – patjo. **Page 12–13:** *Reindeer* – V. Belov, *Wolverine* – Nazzu, *Minke Whale* – Joanne Weston, *Lemming* – BMJ, *Musk Ox* – l i g h t p o e t, *Puffin* – orxy. **Page 14–15:** *Imperial eagle* – Vladimir Kogan Michael, *Purple heron* – Mircea BEZERGHEANU, *Spanish ibex* – Andrew M. Allport, *Whale watching* – Chris Roe, *Dormouse* – Miroslav Hlavko, *Migrating Birds* – Det-anan, *Leaping Salmon* – Krasowit, *River with Salmon* – Sekar B. **Page 16–17:** *European Biso*n – aleksandr hunta, *Alpine Marmot* – Martin Lehmann, *Barn owl* – Mark Bridger, *Eurasian otter* – hfuchs, *Swallow* – seeyou, *Foxes* – Menno Schaefer, *Eurasian lynx* – Bildagentur Zoonar GmbH, *Fire salamander* – Dani Vincek, *Fallow deer* – Budimir Jevtic. **Page 18–19:** *Butcher bird* – Glenn Price, *Loggerhead turtle* – Benjamin Albiach Galan, *Monk seal* – burnel1, *Hermann's tortoise* – Eric Isselee, *Stork* – Marisa Estivill, *Wolf* – davemhuntphotography, *Squirrel* – Menno Schaefer. **Page 20–21:** *Siberian tiger* – davemhuntphotography, *Brown bear* – Eric Isselee, *Siberian crane* – Vishnevskiy Vasily, *Baikal seal* – withGod, *Yakut horse* – Makarova Viktoria, *Great bustard* – Bildagentur Zoonar GmbH, *Pine marten* – Eric Isselee, *Lake Baikal* – Katvic, *Fish owl* – pzAxe. **Page 22–23:** *Roe deer* – Jakub Mrocek, *Black woodpecker* – Bildagentur Zoonar GmbH, *Long-eared bat* – BMJ, *Tawny owl* – Neil Burton, *Crossbill* – Robert L Kothenbeutel, *Eurasian badger* – IVL, *Hedgehog* – Mr. SUTTIPON YAKHAM, *Eurasian jay* – Neil Burton, *European mole* – tchara, *Wild boar* – Tomas K, *Woodland background* – alexey sazonov. **Page 24–25:** *Tropical crab* – haveseen, *Big horn sheep* – MountainHardcore, *Porcupine* – Debbie Steinhausser, *Prairie landscape* – Galyna Andrushko, *Prairie dog* – Mircea BEZERGHEANU, *Desert landscape* – Anton Foltin, *Rattlesnake* – Eric Isselee, *Ocean* – Iakov Kalinin, *Blue fin tuna* – holbox. **Page 26–27:** *Beaver* – Jody Ann, *Moose* – Tom Reichner, *Mountain goat* – Josh Schutz, *Great horned owl* – jadimages, *Mountain lion* – outdoorsman, *Grizzly Bear* – Galyna Andrushko, *Salmon* – Sekar B, *Orca* – Menno Schaefer. **Page 28–29:** *Bald eagle* – Kevin Le, *Monarch butterfly* – BOONCHUAY PROMJIAM, *Raccoon* – Songquan Deng, *Grey whale* – James Michael Dorsey, *American black bear* – nattanan726, *Condor* – Iakov Filimonov, *Acorn woodpecker* – Dennis Donohue, *American bison* – David Osborn. **Page 30–31:** *Everglade background* – shaferaphoto, *Alligator* – jo Crebbin, *Pelican* – jo Crebbin, *Manatee* – Greg Amptman, *Spoonbill* – Agustin Esmoris, *Panther* – jo Crebbin, *Sheepshead fish* – Peter Leahy, *Snail kite* – Rob Stokes, *Apple snail* – Sanit Fuangnakhon, *Mangrove tree crab* – Microstock Man, *Alligator smiling* – Mighty Sequoia Studio. **Page 32–33:** *Desert background* – Anton Foltin, *Desert bee* – Orange Line Media, *Jackrabbit* – Sumikophoto, *Tarantula* – Eric Isselee, *Swallowtail* – Phase4Studios , *Vulture* – claffra, *Gila monster* – fivespots, *Road runner* – Sekar B, *Sidewinder* – fivespots, *Woodpecker* – tntphototravis, *Dried earth* – WitthayaP. **Page 34–35:** *Condor* – vitmark, *Butterfly* – Arvind Balaraman, *Chinchilla* – Robert Eastman, *Mountain range* – Vladimir Sevrinovsky, *Scorpion* – Audrey Snider-Bell, *Dolphin* – guentermanaus, *Turtle* – Rich Carey, *Coral background* – Vilainecrevette. **Page 36–37:** *Rainforest background* – guentermanaus, *Toucan* – Oleksiy Mark, *Macaw* – Super Prin, *Frog* – Aleksey Stemmer, *Anaconda* – Cromagnon, *Anteater* – Joe McDonald, *Sloth* – worldswildlewonders, *Eagle* – MarcusVDT, *Capybara* – Stephen Meese, *Jaguar* – Ana Vasileva, *Tamarin* – Eric Gevaert, *Trees cut down* – PhilipYb. **Page 38–39:** *Island background* – sunsinger, *Finch* – Ryan M. Bolton, *Tortoise* – sunsinger, *Iguana* – Ryan M. Bolton, *Cormorant* – Stubblefield Photography, *Booby* – BlueOrange Studio, *Fur seal* – Pablo Hidalgo, *Lizard* – Stacy Funderburke, *Crab* – Stacy Funderburke, *Penguin* – Elena Kalistratova, *Pelican on rock* – SidEcuador. **Page 40–41:** *Meerkats* – tratong, *Rainforest* – brodtcast, *Camels* – Volker Golzheim, *Elephant* – Graeme Shannon, *Grassland* – Ewan Chesser, *Giraffes* – Janvdb95. **Page 42–43:** *Jerboa* – Geo-Zlat, *Dung beetle* – efendy, *Crocodile* – Mark Caunt, *Wolf* – Alberto Loyo, *Viper* – Eric Isselee, *Scorpion* – Dennis W. Donohue, *Camel* – Wolfgang Zwanzger. **Page 44–45:** *Chameleon* – Cathy Keifer, *Shoebill* – Ekaterina Pokrovsky, *Bat* – Panu Ruangjan, *Pangolin* – Andre Coetzer, *Chimpanzees* – Sergey Uryadnikov, *Gorilla* – David Dea, *Lemur* – apiguide. **Page 46–47:** *Savannah background* – Eduard Kyslynskyy, *Elephant* – Chris Fourie, *Lion* – Eric Isselee, *Wildebeest* – AndreAnita, *Hippopotamus* – apple2499, *Giraffe* – Christian Musat, *Hyena* – bonga1965, *Zebras* – BOONCHUAY PROMJIAM, *Rhinoceros* – Chris Humphries, *Hippo mouth open* – apple2499. **Page 48–49:** *Wading crane* – Super Prin, *Snow leopards* – bigfatcat, *Bactrian camel* – Pichugin Dmitry, *Yak* – Daniel Prudek, *Clown triggerfish* – bluehand, *Sumatran tiger* – Dikky Oesin. **Page 50–51:** *Arabian horse* – Girod-B. Lorelei, *Vulture* – Nazzu, *Hamster* – stock_shot, *Caracal* – Stuart G Porter, *Oryx* – Max Earey, *Bat* – Ivan Kuzmin, *Ibex* – Dmitri Gomon, *Leopard* – kojik, *Baboons* – Fulcanelli. **Page 52–53:** *Antelope* – Vladimir Sevrinovsky, *Polecat* – Zhiltsov Alexandr, *Falcon* – Chris Hill, *Man with eagle* – Pichugin Dmitry, *Marmot* – tantrik71, *Snow Leopard* – Jeannette Katzir Photog, *Partridge* – M.Khebra, *Fox* – schankz. **Page 54–55:** *Bengal tiger* – davemhuntphotography, *Hornbill* – Worraket, *Cobra* – Eric Isselee, *Peacock* – Shawn Hempel, *Markhor* – Volodymyr Burdiak, *Rhinoceros* – ilovezion, *Buffalo* – Hugh Lansdown, *Mynah bird* – grass-lifeisgood, *Elephants* – Ekkachai. **Page 56–57:** *Yak* – eAlisa, *Alligator* – Daniele Pietrobelli, *Golden monkey* – JTang, *Horses* – Anita Huszti, *Cranes* – Erni, *Pheasant* – SergeBertasiusPhotography, *Macaques* – redswept, *Pandas* – Eric Isselee. **Page 58-59:** *Eagle* – Edwin Verin, *Slow loris* – warmer, *Orangutan* – Kjersti Joergensen, *Tapir* – Christian Musat, *Flying lemur* – Vincent St. Thomas, *Rhinoceros* – Judy Whitton, *Praying mantis* – anat chant, *Komodo dragon* – Anna Kucherova. **Page 60–61:** *Ocean background* – Rich Carey, *Jellyfish* – pan demin, *Whale shark* – Krzysztof Odziomek, *Sea cucumber* – orlandin, *Humpback whale* – David Ashley, *Manta ray* – haveseen, *Cuttlefish* – Andrea Izzotti, *Plankton* – Johnlips, *Frogfish* – Silke Baron, *Octopus* – Boris Pamikov, *Mudskipper* – Rich Carey. **Page 62–63:** *Climate image* – CristinaMuraca, *Mountain* – CristinaMuraca, *Rainforest image* – Janelle Lugge, *Tree kangaroo* – Dan Kosmayer, *Ocean image* – gary yim, *Box jellyfish* – almondd, *Desert image* – CristinaMuraca, *Thorny devil lizard* – Janelle Lugge. **Page 64–65:** *Koala* – rickyd, *Funnel-web spider* – James van den Broek, *Kiwi* – Eric Isselee, *Tasmanian devil* – Flash-ka, *Platypus* – worldswildlewonders, *Tuatara* – CreativeNature R.Zwerver, *Frilled lizard* – Matt Cornish, *Saltwater crocodile* – bikeriderlondon. **Page 66–67:** *Reef background* – Andrey_Kuzmin, *Single coral* – skyhyun, *Coral reef* – Jolanta Wojcicka, *Pink coral* – Le Do, *Anemone* – Joe Belanger, *Clown fish* – Jung Hsuan, *Porcupine fish* – Peter Leahy, *Porcupine fish inflated* – Beth Swanson, *Parrot fish* – Cigdem Sean Cooper, *Seahorse* – phugunfire, *Barracuda* – aquapix, *Reef shark* – cbpix, *Lion fish* – puwanai, *Angel fish* – serg_dibrova, *Cleaner fish* – Levent Konuk, *Moray eel* – Richard Whitcombe. **Page 68–69:** *Krill* – Dmytro Pylypenko, *Penguin and seal* – Petra Christen, *Blue whale* – Sebastien Burel, *Squid* – LehaKoK, *Albatross* – Neil Burton, *Penguins* – Footage.Pro, *Antarctic icefish* – Evlakhov Valeriy, *Icefish background* – Vladimir Gjorgiev, *Seal* – Steven Gill. **Page 70–71:** *Prairie dog group* – Henk Bentlage **Back endpaper:** *Tuna* – holbox, *Big horned sheep* – Christopher Gardiner, *Orca* – Xavier MARCHANT, *Young wild boar* – Eric Isselee, *Swallow* – seeyou, *Turtle* – Rich Carey, *Wolf* – davemhuntphotography, *Mink* – Eric Isselee, *Tern* – Menno Schaefer, *Partridge* – M.Khebra, *Triggerfish* – bluehand, *Elephant* – Chris Fourie, *Kiwi* – Eric Isselee.

15 1

Printed in Malaysia

Contents

**Abbreviations
used in this book**

°C	degrees Celsius
mm	millimetre
cm	centimetre
m	metre
km	kilometre
kg	kilogram

Amazing Animals

Animals live in almost every place on Earth. On each continent, separated by oceans and mountains, animals have evolved and adapted in an amazing variety of ways to suit their environment. For example, in polar regions, seals and polar bears grow double layers of fat and fur as protection from freezing temperatures. Animals that have not been able to adapt have died out, or become 'extinct'.

Habitats

A habitat is a place where an animal lives – it can be huge like the ocean or the rainforest or tiny like the underside of a leaf or stone. Tiny habitats are known as micro-habitats.

Adaptations

Each animal is uniquely adapted to the habitat in which it lives. Some animals can live only in one particular habitat, but others can live across many different habitats, for example, foxes can be found in the Arctic and in the hot Sahara Desert.

Fennec foxes are the colour of the desert sand where they live.

Arctic foxes grow a white coat for camouflage against the snow.

Biomes

Biologists have divided the world into different biomes (or zones) that are determined by the climate, landscape and plants that grow there. These include tropical rainforests, grasslands, deserts and mangroves – there are many others. The world map at the front of this book shows the main biomes.

How many species are there?

Over two million species of living things have been described and named by scientists, though many believe the actual figure, including animals we have not yet discovered, could be many times more than this. New species are being discovered every day in remote areas in tropical rainforests or deep in the dark oceans.

Classification

We can sort (classify) animals into groups, according to their distinct features. For example:

Cephalopods are molluscs with a large head and tentacles.

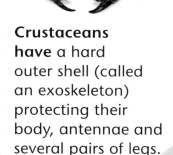

Crustaceans have a hard outer shell (called an exoskeleton) protecting their body, antennae and several pairs of legs.

Birds are warm-blooded animals with two legs, wings, a beak and feathers. They lay eggs from which their young hatch. Most birds can fly.

Molluscs are animals with a soft body and, often, a protective shell.

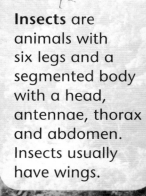

Insects are animals with six legs and a segmented body with a head, antennae, thorax and abdomen. Insects usually have wings.

Fish are cold-blooded animals that breathe through gills, have scales and fins, and live in water.

Arachnids have eight legs and a body divided into two segments.

Mammals are warm-blooded animals that have fur or hair. They give birth to live young and produce milk to feed them.

Reptiles are cold-blooded animals that have scaly skin and, like birds, lay eggs from which their young hatch.

Amphibians are cold-blooded animals that breed in water but as adults spend time on land.

Living Together

There are two main types of animals: vertebrates and invertebrates.

Vertebrates

are animals with a backbone. Mammals, reptiles, amphibians, birds and fish are vertebrates.

Invertebrates

are animals without a backbone. Insects, worms, snails and spiders are invertebrates.

We can also classify animals according to their diet.

Herbivores eat plants.

Carnivores eat other animals.

Omnivores eat both plants and other animals.

Food chains

Food chains are used to show how each living thing gets its food. Animals that feed on other animals are called 'predators'. The animals they eat are called 'prey'. Food chains always start with plants because plants can produce their own food, by photosynthesis, using energy from the sun.

PLANT
(producer)

CATERPILLAR
(consumer)

BLUE TIT
(consumer)

SPARROW HAWK
(consumer)

If one link in the food chain is broken, for example, if the trees in a forest are cut down and cleared, many of the animals that feed on those plants will die and this will affect all the other animals in the chain.

Plants and animals need each other for survival. Plants provide food and shelter for animals. In return, animals help to spread pollen and scatter plant seeds.

Changing world

The Earth is getting warmer, seas are rising and the polar ice caps are melting. The world's population is growing – by 2050 there will be 10 billion people. Industry, farming and mining are expanding to meet the increased need for housing, food and manufactured goods. These changes are resulting in wide-scale habitat loss: species of plants and animals are being threatened on a scale never before experienced.

Threats to life

In every country in the world species of animals are threatened with extinction. Some of these are shown in this atlas. The symbols in the key below identify their current conservation status.

We know that animals can evolve and adapt to changing environments, but this process takes time – it can take hundreds or thousands of years.

The future
What can we do to help save the Earth's endangered animals?

Education – scientists say we need to learn more about the problems that the Earth will face if we continue to lose animal and plant species. The more we know, the better we can protect our living world.

Protection – some scientists and conservationists say we need to give greater protection to endangered species by stopping poachers and hunters, reducing pollution, and by preserving wilderness habitats.

VU VULNERABLE
The polar bear is unlikely to adapt before the Arctic ice thaws.

EN ENDANGERED
The golden lion tamarin is endangered due to the loss of its habitat.

WANT TO **KNOW MORE?**

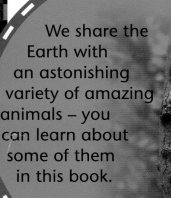

We share the Earth with an astonishing variety of amazing animals – you can learn about some of them in this book.

The Arctic

People and animals living in the Arctic have adapted to cool summers and long, cold winters when temperatures fall as low as –40 °C. The Arctic region is a huge frozen sea covered in floating ice and surrounded by a treeless frozen landscape called 'tundra'. But global warming is changing the Arctic – the sea ice is melting and animals that hunt on the ice, such as the polar bear, are threatened with extinction.

Arctic Circle
Bering Strait
CANADA
USA (Alaska)
Chukchi Sea
Limit of permanent ice cap
East Siberian Sea
RUSSIA
Beaufort Sea
New Siberian Islands
ARCTIC OCEAN
Laptev Sea
Victoria Island
North Pole
Kara Sea
Ellesmere Island
Franz Josef Land
Novaya Zemlya
Baffin Island
Baffin Bay
Wandel Sea
Svalbard (NORWAY)
GREENLAND (DENMARK)
Greenland Sea
Barents Sea
North Cape
Norwegian Sea
NORWAY
FINLAND
Arctic Circle
ICELAND

Arctic fox and hare

In summer, the fur of the Arctic fox and hare is brown. Each winter, it changes to white to better camouflage against the snow.

Arctic tern

This small bird is famous for flying from pole to pole so that it can enjoy two summers every year! It sets off from Greenland in September and heads for Antarctica to spend the summer there, before migrating back to Greenland in May to breed.

| 0 | miles | 1000 |
| 0 | km | 1000 |

(VU)

Polar bear

The Arctic thaw is endangering the polar bear to the point where there will be none left in the wild by 2050. Polar bears hunt seals from the ice. They are excellent swimmers but can't swim continuously, so they stop to rest on the ice. If there is no ice to rest on then they will drown.

Beluga whale

This white 'canary of the sea' communicates with its voice in underwater songs and always seems to be smiling! Belugas group in huge herds for breeding.

Killer whale

The orca, or killer whale, is a cousin of the dolphin. It feeds on seals, squid and fish. Hunting in pods of up to 40 whales, orcas circle and trap their prey.

Walrus

Walruses have two big tusks that they use to haul themselves out of the water and to defend themselves from rivals. They have thick layers of fat as insulation from the freezing Arctic temperatures.

WANT TO KNOW MORE?

North of the Arctic Circle there are 24 hours of daylight on midsummer's day but on midwinter's day it is completely dark for 24 hours.

Lion's mane jellyfish

It has neither brains nor bones, but hundreds of poisonous tentacles instead. The tentacles, like long hairs, are almost invisible in the water so it is easy for a fish or other jellyfish to get stung by them.

Europe

The continent of Europe is small, but it has a large population of over 730 million people. In the north, Europe reaches up as far as the Arctic Circle and in the south stretches down to the Mediterranean Sea. The Atlantic Ocean is on its western coastline while in the east the Ural Mountains form a natural boundary.

ICELAND

Climate

Europe has a temperate climate with long hot summers in the southern Mediterranean countries and long cold winters in the north and east. The Gulf Stream warms the western islands while eastern countries feel the bitter chill of the Siberian wind.

Forests

Thousands of years ago northern Europe was covered by dense forests which thrived in its mild, wet climate. As Europe's human population grew, many trees were cleared to make way for agriculture and industry. Despite this, forests still make up about one quarter of the land area. The coniferous forests of Scandinavia and Russia are home to a variety of animals including elk, wolves and wild boar.

Mountains

Europe's highest mountains, the Pyrenees and the Alps, protect the south from the cold and rain. Agile antelopes, called chamois, roam the high mountains in summer, leaping across rocks to escape from predatory bears and lynx. With its speed and strong legs, the chamois can make a quick escape.

North Sea

WESTERN EUROPE

Mediter Se

AFRICA

Domestic animals

Europe's animals have learned to live alongside people. Many have been domesticated as pets or farm animals. Pigs, poultry, sheep, goats and herds of dairy cows are a familiar sight as they graze on lush green farm pastures.

ARCTIC OCEAN

Arctic Circle

NORTHERN EUROPE

RUSSIA

CENTRAL EUROPE

SOUTHEAST EUROPE

Black Sea

ASIA

Wild animals

There are few remaining wilderness areas left in Europe and yet you can still find rare and amazing animals. In the marshlands of southern France you may see the wild Camargue horses roaming freely. These small white horses, once domesticated, have now been returned to the wild.

Oceans

Common and grey seals, porpoises and bottlenose dolphins are regularly seen around the European coasts. Bottlenose dolphins are social and intelligent mammals. They live in groups and communicate with each other using clicking noises. They feed on fish, squid and shrimps.

Northern Europe

The landscape of northern Europe has been shaped by ancient glaciers, or rivers of ice. As the ice melted in parts of Norway and Iceland, it moved down the mountains, carving many lakes and narrow steep-sided fjords down to the sea. The natural landscape of this region, with its high mountains, dense forests, lakes, rivers and seas, is relatively unspoilt compared with the rest of Europe.

Greenland Sea · Arctic Circle
ICELAND
Reykjavik
ATLANTIC OCEAN

FAEROE ISLANDS (Denmark)
Torshavn

ARCTIC OCEAN

Barents Sea

RUSSIA

LAPLAND

Kebnekaise 2106m

Arctic Circle

Kemijoki

Norwegian Sea

N O R W A Y

S W E D E N

F I N L A N D

Saimaa

Gulf of Bothnia

Sognefjorden

Glomma

Klarälven

Dalälven

Oslo

Vänern

Vättern

Stockholm

Helsinki

Gulf of Finland

Tallinn

ESTONIA

Skagerrak

Gotland

North Sea

LATVIA

Riga

Western Dvina

DENMARK

Copenhagen

Baltic Sea

RUSSIA

Bornholm

KALININGRAD (Russia)

LITHUANIA

Vilnius

BELARUS

GERMANY

POLAND

0   miles   200

0   km   200

Reindeer (known as caribou in America)

In Norway, Sweden and Finland herds of wild and domesticated reindeer are kept for milk, meat and skins. They spend the summer grazing on pastures near the coast, and the long winters inland. They eat three times as much in summer as they do in winter, when pastures are often covered in snow. Both males and females grow antlers, though the males' antlers tend to be larger.

Wolverine

A wolverine could make a meal of a lemming, or even a reindeer. It is a fierce predator, and belongs to the weasel family – although it looks like a small bear. It lives alone in remote forests or tundra habitats.

Minke whale

Minke whales are often seen on whale-watching cruises in the north Atlantic, where they are fairly numerous. Norway has traditionally hunted the minke whale to keep down whale numbers and so maintain supplies of fish for humans. Some people say this is wrong, and that whale hunting is a cruel activity.

Lemming

Related to other rodents such as rats, mice and hamsters, the lemming is found in or near the Arctic in tundra habitats. It will sometimes show aggression to predators and humans as a warning signal. Lemmings follow their strong biological urge to migrate in large numbers.

Musk ox

This big, hairy animal eats only plants, roots, mosses and flowers. It is a protected species in Norway. It has two layers of fur – a shorter insulating layer that it sheds in summer and a longer layer that it keeps all year.

Puffin

The Atlantic puffin's beak has a bright orange layer that it grows to attract a mate. After breeding, it sheds this part of its beak. Puffins can swim underwater to collect sand eels from the sea bed.

Western Europe

Farmland, industry, cities and towns cover a large part of western Europe. The animals that live here have for centuries had a close relationship with people. In the north, there are herds of farm animals, such as sheep and cattle, grazing on rich green pastures. In the south, there is one of the world's most important nature reserves – the Coto Doñana in Spain.

Map labels

Shetland Islands
Orkney Islands
Outer Hebrides
ATLANTIC OCEAN
SCOTLAND
Edinburgh
NORTHERN IRELAND
Belfast
Dublin
IRELAND
UNITED KINGDOM
WALES
Cardiff
ENGLAND
London
Thames
North Sea
NETHERLANDS
The Hague
Amsterdam
GERMANY
English Channel
Brussels
BELGIUM
LUXEMBOURG
Luxembourg
Seine
Paris
Loire
FRANCE
SWITZERLA
Mt Blanc 4810m
ALPS
ITALY
Bay of Biscay
Dordogne
Garonne
MASSIF CENTRAL
Rhone
MONACO
PYRENEES
ANDORRA
Ebro
Duero
Madrid
SPAIN
Corsica
Mediterranean Sea
PORTUGAL
Tagus
Lisbon
Guadalquivir
Coto Doñana
Gibraltar (to UK)
Balearic Islands

miles 200
km 200

Azores (to Portugal)
ATLANTIC OCEAN
SPAIN
PORTUGAL
Madeira (to Portugal)
Canary Islands (to Spain)
W. SAHARA
MOROCCO
miles 400
km 400

Purple heron

The purple heron spends the winter in Africa and breeds in the summer in the lakes and marshlands of the Camargue in southern France, where the River Rhone reaches the Mediterranean Sea. It stands in shallow waters, waiting for prey such as fish, frogs and small birds.

Iberian imperial eagle

Flocks of flamingos, spoonbills, kites and other migratory birds can be spotted in the marshes, dunes and woodlands of the Coto Doñana, as well as endangered species such as the Spanish lynx and this Iberian imperial eagle.

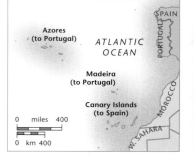

VU

Whale watching

The countries of western Europe are surrounded by sea. Whales can be seen along the Atlantic coasts and in the Mediterranean Sea, especially the minke whale. Minke whales travel in small pods of two or three whales. Occasionally, humpback and fin whales are spotted in the North Sea.

Spanish ibex

A rare wild goat, the Spanish ibex climbs and jumps expertly off rocky ledges and steep slopes in the mountains of Spain. Males are much bigger than females and have longer horns.

WANT TO KNOW MORE?

Using rising air currents, known as 'thermals', migrating birds can glide to conserve energy on long flights. Thermals work best in hilly country so the mountains of the Sierra Nevada in Spain and the North African Atlas range are staging posts for queuing migrants heading north or south.

Endangered species

The protection of endangered species is a high priority in Europe. It is thanks to protection that the golden eagle, once hunted almost to extinction, is starting to increase in numbers again. Other protected European species include the brown bear, the natterjack toad and the dormouse.

EN

Atlantic salmon

Atlantic salmon migrate over long distances from the ocean to rivers where they spawn (lay their eggs). They swim upriver, often returning to the same place where they were born. After laying their eggs most salmon will die, and so the life cycle begins again.

Central Europe

A region of contrasts, central Europe extends from fertile farmland in the north to dry shrub and scrubland in the south of the region. Across the middle, running from west to east, there are mountain habitats in the Alps and the Carpathian mountains. Many animals living in central Europe have had to adapt to a human population taking over their habitat.

DENMARK
Baltic Sea
LITHUANIA
RUSSIA
BELARUS
NETHERLANDS
Elbe
NORTH EUROPEAN PLAIN
Vistula
Berlin
Warsaw
BELGIUM
GERMANY
Elbe
Oder
POLAND
LUXEMBOURG
Rhine
Prague
CZECH
REPUBLIC
CARPATHIAN
MOUNTAINS
UKRAINE
FRANCE
Danube
SLOVAKIA
BLACK
FOREST
Vienna
Bratislava
AUSTRIA
Bern
LIECHTENSTEIN
Drau
HUNGARY
Lake Geneva
SWITZERLAND
ALPS
Mt Blanc
4810m
Lake
Garda
SLOVENIA
Ljubljana
CROATIA
Po
Po Valley
MONACO
APENNINES
SAN MARINO
Ligurian
Sea
Adriatic Sea
0   miles   200
0   km   200
Corsica
(FRANCE)
VATICAN CITY
Tiber
Rome
ITALY
Sardinia
Tyrrhenian
Sea
Ionian
Sea
Mediterranean Sea
Sicily
Mount Etna
3340m
MALTA
Valletta

European bison

This bison may be a big beast but it eats only leaves, bark and twigs. It once roamed throughout Europe but today it is found only in one forest on the border of Poland and Belarus. There are now fewer than 500 of these bison alive in the wild.

Alpine marmot

The marmot looks like an overweight squirrel! In the summer months it feeds on the seeds, berries and fruits of the forest to build up stores of body fat in readiness for hibernation. Marmots live in family groups in deep burrows in the ground.

Barn owl

The barn owl has a distinctive heart-shaped face. It hunts its prey, mainly rodents, at night. It can't see them in the darkness but it can hear them. Hovering a few metres above the ground, the barn owl pinpoints the exact location of its prey then drops down silently for the kill.

Eurasian otter

Otters have long, tapering bodies and webbed feet. They are expert swimmers and feed on fish and frogs in rivers and lakes, but occasionally they manage to catch rabbits on land. Otter numbers are increasing as pollutants are being cleaned from rivers.

Swallow

The swallow is a master of aerobatics. It swoops, dives, twists and turns to catch an insect-meal in mid-air. Swallows make their nests from mud that they fasten to the walls of buildings and under roofs. Male swallows will attract a mate by singing and showing off their flying skills.

EN

Eurasian lynx

The tufted ears of the lynx make it different from other wild cats. Lynx have been hunted in the past, so that today in the high mountain forests of the Alps there are only about 100 left. Lynx live and hunt alone, mainly at night, by stalking and sneaking up on their prey of small mammals and birds.

Fallow deer

Fallow deer have spotted coats and flat-topped antlers. They live in woodlands and on farmland. Adult males live alone, while females live in herds. Males use their impressive antlers to fight for females in the breeding season.

WANT TO KNOW MORE?

European animals are often found living in or on the edge of urban environments. For example, many foxes live in towns and cities, where they survive by eating food scraps from dustbins.

Fire salamander

The yellow and black fire salamander has a poisonous skin that burns any animal that tries to eat it! These salamanders live in damp habitats near streams and give birth to live young in the water. They eat worms, which they hunt after the rain.

Southeast Europe

Farming has always been important in the countries of southeast Europe. The countries that cluster around the Adriatic and the Mediterranean seas are mountainous, with hot, dry summers and mild winters. Countries further north, such as Ukraine and Belarus, have warm summers but much colder winters.

LATVIA
LITHUANIA
Minsk
BELARUS
Dnieper
Pripet
RUSSIA
Pripet Marshes
Kiev
UKRAINE
Donets
POLAND
Dnieper
SLOVAKIA
CARPATHIAN MOUNTAINS
Dniester
MOLDOVA
Southern Bug
Prut
Chisinau
Sea of Azov
AUSTRIA
Budapest
Tisza
HUNGARY
Transylvania
SLOVENIA
Zagreb
CROATIA
Sava
ROMANIA
Crimea
Belgrade
TRANSYLVANIAN ALPS
Black Sea
BOSNIA & HERZEGOVINA
Bucharest
Sarajevo
SERBIA
Danube
BULGARIA
Adriatic Sea
Dalmatia
MONTENEGRO
Pristina
BALKAN MOUNTAINS
Podgorica
KOSOVO
Sofia
Rhodope
▲ Musala, 2925m
Mountains
Tirana
Skopje
MACEDONIA
TURKEY
Lake Ohrid
Lake Prespa
ALBANIA
Corfu
Pindos Mountains
GREECE
Lesbos
Ionian Sea
Aegean Sea
TURKEY
Athens
Peloponnese
Mediterranean Sea
Cyclades
Dodecanese
Sea of Crete
Rhodes
Crete

0   miles   200
0   km   200

Butcher bird

The predatory birdlife of southern Europe has adapted to catching creatures such as grasshoppers, bees, small lizards and snakes. There are birds such as shrikes (or butcher birds) that skewer their prey on thorny branches and bee-eaters that hit their prey (bees) against a hard surface to remove the sting before eating them!

Loggerhead turtle

EN

Female turtles migrate thousands of kilometres to lay their eggs. When night-time falls, they dig a hole on the beach in which they lay more than a hundred eggs! Then they cover them with sand and head back to the sea. The baby turtles hatch two months later and make a dash for the water before seagulls can snatch them up.

Hermann's tortoise

Found throughout southern Europe, this tortoise has a black and yellow patterned shell. It has no teeth but uses its sharp jaws to bite at leaves, flowers and fruits. It digs a hole in which to hibernate through the winter months.

WANT TO **KNOW MORE?**

Southern Europe was once covered in trees but now it is mostly shrub and scrubland with pines and cypress trees providing food and homes for nesting birds, red squirrels and insects.

White stork

During springtime, the bee-eater and many birds including eagles migrate north to cooler regions while birds such as the stork arrive to nest and breed. Storks mate for life, returning to the same nest site each year. The white stork can travel up to 20,000 km a year between Europe and Africa!

Grey wolf

Once found all over Europe, the grey wolf is now a protected species in many countries. A top predator with only humans to fear, the grey wolf is about the size of a German Shepherd dog. It lives in families, feeding mainly on livestock and small mammals.

Russia

Russia stretches from frozen coniferous forests in the north at the Arctic Circle, through the Siberian plateau in the centre, to the steppes and mountains bordering Mongolia in the south. In Siberia, Lake Baikal is the oldest and deepest lake on Earth.

Siberian tiger

Also known as the Amur tiger, the Siberian tiger lives in the birch forests of eastern Russia. They are the largest of all wild cats. There are more in captivity in zoos than living in the wild, where there are only about 400 left. They hunt at night for elk and wild boar.

Baikal seal

This small seal lives only in Lake Baikal, where it feeds on the golomyanka fish, or 'oilfish'. It is a mystery how this seal got here so far from the sea, but it is thought that millions of years ago the lake and the sea may have been connected.

Brown bear

In the spring, Siberian brown bears come down from the mountains to feed on caddisflies, berries, bulbs, roots and small mammals on the shores of Lake Baikal. They are small compared to their cousins, the grizzly bears, found in North America.

Great bustard

In the south of Russia, on flat grassland (or steppe), the great bustard spends the summer. With its large, barrel-shaped chest, the male is one of the heaviest flying birds!

Siberian crane

Snowy white Siberian cranes migrate from eastern Russia to China for the winter. They are omnivores, feeding mainly on plants, worms and fish. Serrated edges on their beaks help them hold on to prey.

CR

Pine marten

About the same size as a pet cat, the pine marten can climb and run along tree branches in pursuit of its prey, which includes squirrels, birds and insects. It hunts mainly at dusk and at night. Foxes, eagles and people are its main threat.

WANT TO KNOW MORE?

Lake Baikal holds 20% of the world's freshwater and is home to many unique creatures. It is 1,632 m deep – that's as high as ten skyscrapers placed on top of each other. Scientists think it could be 25 million years old!

Fish owl

With a 2-metre wingspan, this is one of the largest and rarest owls in the world. It breeds in large, old trees that grow along streams in Russia's Far East, where it hunts its favourite prey, salmon.

Yakut horse

This rare horse is adapted to surviving the winter snows of Siberia. Its thick mane and heavy coat provide protection from the cold, and it uses its heavy hooves to uncover grass to eat from deep beneath the snow.

Habitat Focus:
European Woodland

Before people arrived, almost the whole of Europe was covered in trees. Today, the only remaining ancient forests are in the north and in protected areas in Germany, the Carpathians and Poland. These forests are home to large carnivores, such as the rare brown bear, lynx and wolf, as well as roe deer, wild boar, small mammals and song birds.

Roe deer

This small, European deer is rarely seen by people because it is a shy animal that prefers to feed at night. The male has short antlers. The roe deer has a reddish-brown coat in summer that turns to grey for camouflage in winter.

Black woodpecker

The black woodpecker is the largest in Europe, growing up to 55 cm in length. It is all black, save for a red patch on its head. Like other woodpeckers its feet have evolved to help it cling onto tree trunks, with two toes pointing frontwards and two pointing back.

Long-eared bat

With ears as long as its body, this bat flies on leathery wings that stretch out from its arms to its legs. It calls out then listens to the returning echoes to find insect prey.

Tawny owl

The tawny owl has brown or grey feathers. It hunts for small mammals in total darkness using its keen sense of hearing. The male and female have different calls. The female's call is more high-pitched than the male.

Eurasian badger

A black and white stripy head and a long snout distinguish the badger. This nocturnal animal has a varied diet which includes earthworms and insects. Badgers live in burrows called 'setts'.

Hedgehog

Thousands of sharp spikes protect the body of the hedgehog. When threatened by predators, it rolls itself up into a ball to make the spikes stand out. In this defensive position, it is unlikely to get eaten! A hedgehog's diet consists mainly of earthworms and slugs.

Crossbill

Crossbills are colourful finches that live in the tops of trees in the pine forests of Europe. They eat seeds from pine cones, and their bills evolved to be like crossed-over scissors to remove seeds from the cones. Male crossbills are red, and females a yellowy green.

Eurasian jay

Jays bury acorns to eat during the winter. As they sometimes forget where these are buried, this helps oak trees to spread through the forest. Jays also eat eggs, smaller birds and insects.

European mole

This black, furry animal is adapted to spending most of its life underground. It has large front paws suitable for digging tunnels in the soil, but poor eyesight. Earthworms are its main diet. It will patrol its tunnels waiting for them to drop inside.

Wild boar

This large, wild pig called a 'boar' is native to Europe. Using its long snout, big nostrils and keen sense of smell, it can find food buried underground. The young have stripy coats for camouflage against the background of forest plants.

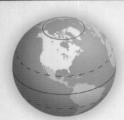

North America

The continent of North America is the third largest in the world. It comprises the USA and Canada, two of the world's biggest countries. It includes different climate zones and habitats, ranging from frozen landscapes in the Arctic to hot deserts and tropical rainforests in the south.

Climate

In the north, in icy Alaska, temperatures stay well below freezing for most of the year, whilst in the south they rise to higher than 49 °C in the Mexican deserts and 33 °C in the tropical islands of the Caribbean.

Forests

Coniferous forests of tall pines, fir and spruce cover large areas in the mountainous north of the continent. These forests are home to many wild animals, including caribou, moose, woodpecker and North American porcupine.

Mountains

The Rocky Mountains extend down the western side of the North American continent, while on the east there are the Appalachians. In these mountain wildernesses, animals such as mountain goats, mountain lions and big horn sheep (left) roam freely.

ARCTY

U S A
(ALASKA)

PACIFIC OCEAN

CANADA

MEXICO

Prairies

In the middle of the North American continent there are grasslands called prairies. The prairies are flat and the soil is perfect for growing wheat, rye, oats and corn. The prairies are home to the prairie dog, a rodent native to North America.

Deserts

In the southwest of the USA and Mexico, in the Mojave and Sonoran deserts, the air is dry and dusty, and rainfall scarce. Desert animals, such as the rattlesnake, survive on the water contained in the food they eat.

Oceans

The Pacific Ocean in the west and Atlantic Ocean in the east are home to a variety of creatures, from sea otters to humpback whales. In the east, a warm current of water known as the Gulf Stream flows northwards, transporting migrating animals such as sharks, turtles and blue fin tuna across the Atlantic.

OCEAN

GREENLAND
(Denmark)

Arctic Circle

ATLANTIC OCEAN

UNITED
STATES
OF
AMERICA

Tropic of Cancer

Caribbean
Sea

CENTRAL AND
SOUTH AMERICA

Canada

The main habitats of Canada are Arctic tundra, coniferous and mixed forests, the Rocky Mountains and Great Lake landscapes. Mining and forestry have led to the extinction of some native animal species, but by setting up of National Wildlife Parks and Migratory Bird Sanctuaries it is hoped that the animals that have made Canada popular with tourists will be protected.

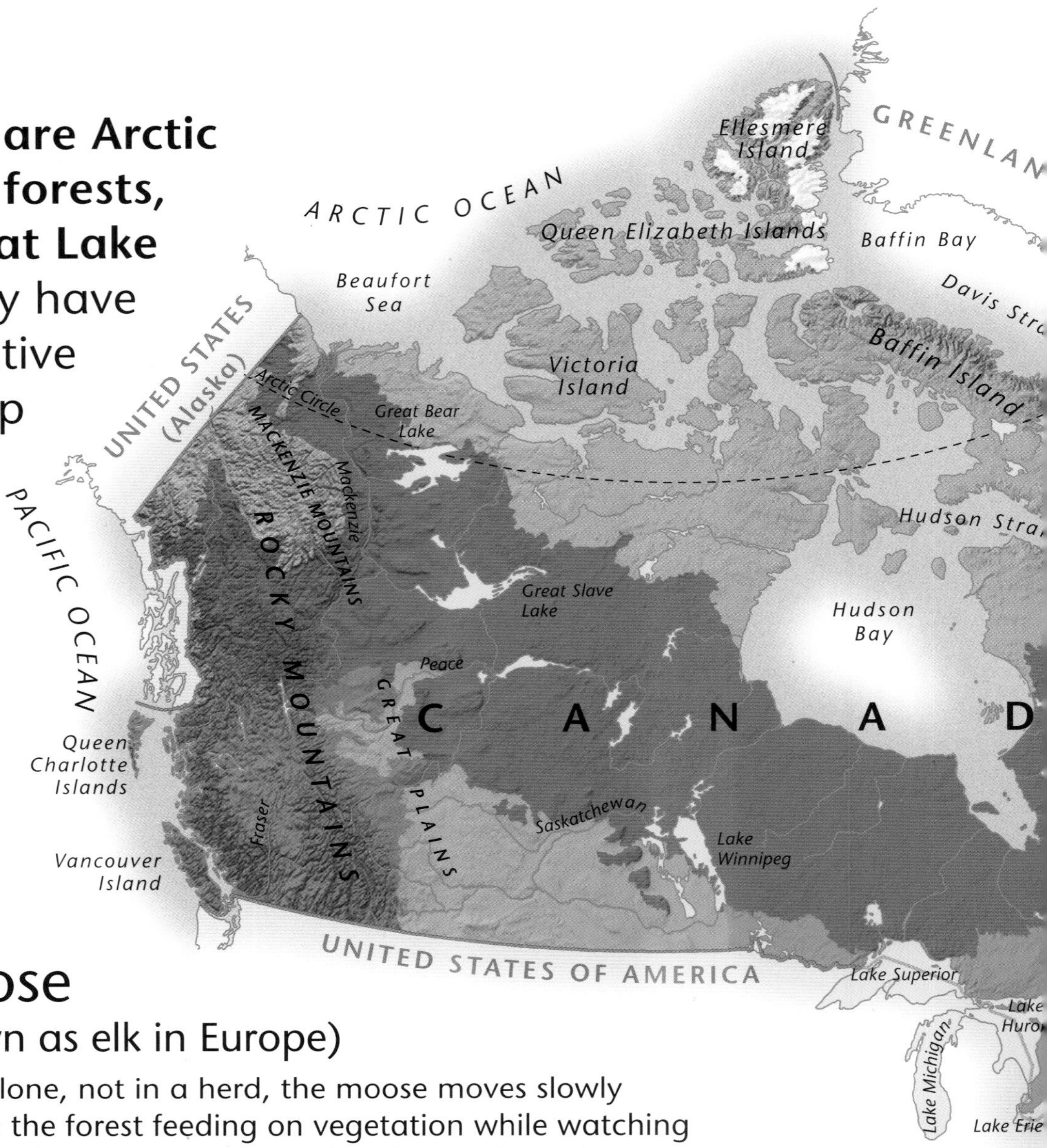

ARCTIC OCEAN
Ellesmere Island
GREENLAN
Queen Elizabeth Islands
Baffin Bay
Beaufort Sea
Davis Stra
Baffin Island
Victoria Island
UNITED STATES (Alaska)
Arctic Circle
Great Bear Lake
MACKENZIE MOUNTAINS
Mackenzie
PACIFIC OCEAN
ROCKY MOUNTAINS
Hudson Stra
Great Slave Lake
Hudson Bay
Peace
GREAT PLAINS
CANAD
Queen Charlotte Islands
Saskatchewan
Fraser
Lake Winnipeg
Vancouver Island
UNITED STATES OF AMERICA
Lake Superior
Lake Huro
Lake Michigan
Lake Erie

Moose

(known as elk in Europe)

Living alone, not in a herd, the moose moves slowly through the forest feeding on vegetation while watching out for wolves, bears and people, who are its main predators. Their impressive antlers are used for defence and when challenging other males in the mating season.

Beaver

One of Canada's national symbols, beavers are large nocturnal rodents, famous for their dam-building skills. They create deep ponds in which to build their homes (called 'lodges') and canals that they use to transport food. Their front teeth grow continuously so that they are not worn down by their diet of bark and leaves.

Rocky mountain goat

Found only in North America, in the Rocky Mountains, this goat climbs confidently over cliffs and ice. Its multi-layered, white woolly coat provides protection from temperatures that can fall as low as –45 °C in winter.

Great horned owl

Also known as the tiger owl, this owl can be recognised by the tufts on its ears. The tufts don't help it to hear, but scientists think they might help with species recognition or even camouflage. This nocturnal bird of prey feeds on smaller birds, small mammals and skunks! It has few predators, apart from people.

Mountain lion

The mountain lion (sometimes called a cougar or puma) lives a solitary life. Avoiding other cats, it is fiercely territorial and will protect its territory from intruders. A carnivore, it eats large mammals such as deer, beavers and raccoons. The young, called kittens, stay with their mother for up to two years.

WANT TO KNOW MORE?

The icy waters of Hudson Bay are home to Arctic cod, salmon and polar plaice. Migrant birds live here during the summer, including snow geese, Canada geese and tundra swans as well as some larger visiting predators – killer whales and belugas.

Labrador Sea

LAURENTIAN MOUNTAINS

Newfoundland

Gulf of St Lawrence

St Lawrence

ATLANTIC OCEAN

0   miles   500

0   km   500

Grizzly bear

A dangerous predator, the grizzly bear lives mainly in forests, eating anything it can find – including this migrating salmon. It can run fast to chase prey and when standing on its hind legs can reach up to 3 m tall.

United States of America

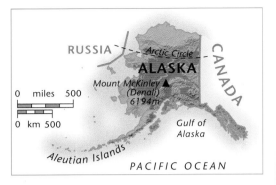

RUSSIA
Arctic Circle
ALASKA
CANADA
Mount McKinley (Denali) 6194m
0 miles 500
0 km 500
Gulf of Alaska
Aleutian Islands
PACIFIC OCEAN

One of the largest countries in the world, the USA is home to 310 million people and a huge range of ecosystems and animals. It has the largest freshwater lake by area in the world and the fourth longest river – the Mississippi. The USA was the first country to set up national parks. One of its parks, Yellowstone, sits on top of a volcanic crater.

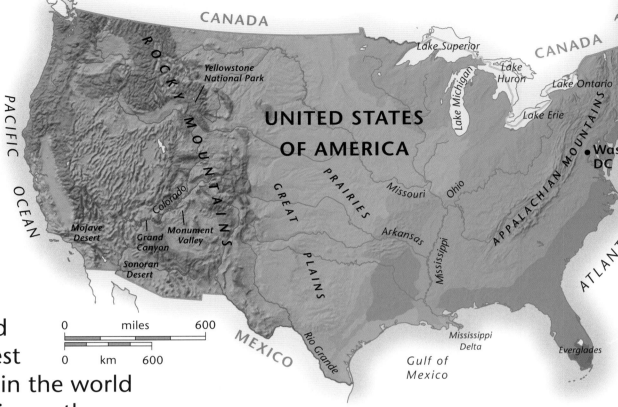

CANADA
Lake Superior
CANADA
Lake Michigan
Lake Huron
Lake Ontario
Lake Erie
UNITED STATES OF AMERICA
ROCKY MOUNTAINS
Yellowstone National Park
PRAIRIES
Missouri
Ohio
APPALACHIAN MOUNTAINS
Was DC
Colorado
GREAT PLAINS
Arkansas
Mississippi
Mojave Desert
Grand Canyon
Monument Valley
Sonoran Desert
ATLANT
0 miles 600
0 km 600
MEXICO
Rio Grande
Mississippi Delta
Everglades
Gulf of Mexico

PACIFIC OCEAN
Kauai
Oahu
Molokai
Honolulu
Lanai
Maui
0 miles 50
0 km 50
Hawaii
HAWAII

Monarch butterfly

Monarch butterflies fly all the way from Canada to spend winter in the warmer climates of California, Mexico and Florida. In the summer, they fly back home to lay their eggs. When the next generation of young butterflies hatch, they will repeat the same journey.

Bald eagle

The national bird of the USA, the bald eagle is not actually bald but has a distinctive white head and tail, and black body feathers. This big bird of prey has a wingspan of up to 2.5 m. It lives near water where it preys mainly on fish and dead animals.

Raccoon

You can recognise a raccoon from the mask of dark fur around its eyes and its striped tail. This nocturnal 'bandit' snatches frogs, mice, insects, birds' eggs, and anything else it can find to eat. Females can have up to seven cubs.

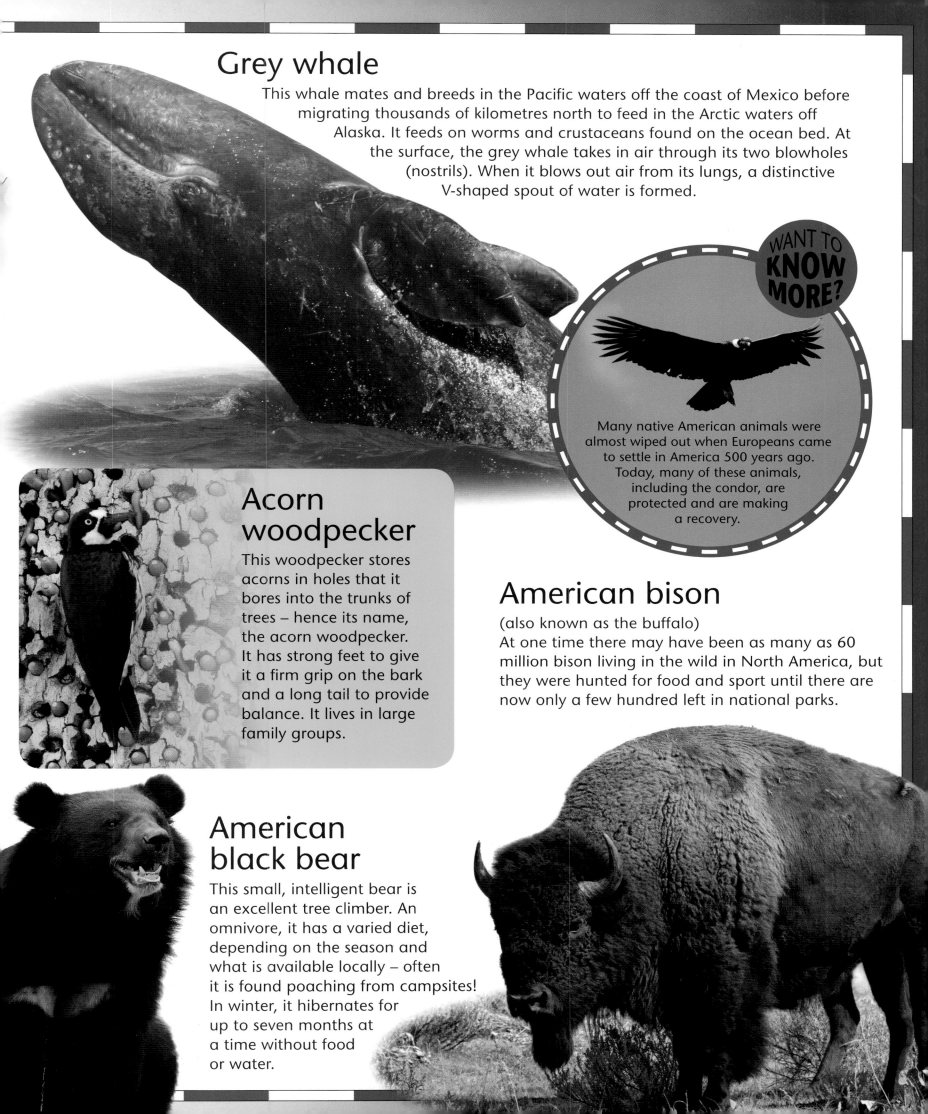

Grey whale

This whale mates and breeds in the Pacific waters off the coast of Mexico before migrating thousands of kilometres north to feed in the Arctic waters off Alaska. It feeds on worms and crustaceans found on the ocean bed. At the surface, the grey whale takes in air through its two blowholes (nostrils). When it blows out air from its lungs, a distinctive V-shaped spout of water is formed.

WANT TO KNOW MORE?

Many native American animals were almost wiped out when Europeans came to settle in America 500 years ago. Today, many of these animals, including the condor, are protected and are making a recovery.

Acorn woodpecker

This woodpecker stores acorns in holes that it bores into the trunks of trees – hence its name, the acorn woodpecker. It has strong feet to give it a firm grip on the bark and a long tail to provide balance. It lives in large family groups.

American bison

(also known as the buffalo)
At one time there may have been as many as 60 million bison living in the wild in North America, but they were hunted for food and sport until there are now only a few hundred left in national parks.

American black bear

This small, intelligent bear is an excellent tree climber. An omnivore, it has a varied diet, depending on the season and what is available locally – often it is found poaching from campsites! In winter, it hibernates for up to seven months at a time without food or water.

Habitat Focus:
Florida Everglades

At the tip of Florida, the Everglades have been described as 'a river of grass flowing to the sea'. This fragile habitat of mangrove swamps and forests is protected by the Everglades National Park. Many endangered species, including the Florida panther and the West Indian manatee, live here.

Brown pelican

The smallest of the pelican family, the brown pelican dives to catch fish in its pouch. It nests in colonies near the water while keeping watch for its main enemy, the alligator. This pelican is a good example of species recovery, as it was once on the brink of extinction.

American alligator

This reptile was hunted for its skin and so became an endangered species but now, with protection, the American alligator has made a great recovery. This top predator can sneak up on its prey, swimming silently, with only its nostrils and eyes breaking the surface of the water!

West Indian manatee

A slow-swimming mammal of rivers and estuaries, the manatee feeds on water plants. It uses its flippers to 'walk' and search for food along the riverbed and steers with its broad, flat tail.

EN

Florida panther

Only about 100 of these rare cats remain. You can find them in the dry lowlands of the Everglades National Park, where they are a protected species. To maintain its health, the Florida panther needs to eat one deer (or 10 raccoons) per week. In the wild, these panthers are preyed upon by alligators.

Roseate spoonbill

This flamboyant-looking pink-feathered bird nests in mangrove shrubs or trees where it lays up to five eggs. The shape of the spoonbill's beak helps it to sift insects, crabs, frogs and fish from the muddy waters. Like a flamingo, it is from this diet that it gets its pink colour.

Sheepshead fish

Fish are the main link in the Everglades food chain because they are food for wading birds, larger fish and alligators. There are close to 300 species of fish in the Everglades, including this sheepshead fish.

WANT TO KNOW MORE?

Alligators are cold-blooded reptiles – this means their body is the same temperature as their surroundings. They like to lie in the sun and don't need to worry about getting sunburnt because they have tough protective scales!

Everglade snail kite

This bird of prey eats apple snails, a type of mollusc found only in the wetlands of Florida. Its curved beak helps this picky eater to prise the snail from

Mangrove tree crab

This crab can climb trees! A small omnivore (it is only about 2 cm long), it feeds on mangrove leaves and lugworms. Black hairs on the ends of its legs help it to grip leaf surfaces, while its speckled shell helps it to blend in with its environment.

Habitat Focus:
Sonoran Desert

The border between the USA and Mexico runs through the Sonoran Desert. Daytime temperatures in summer can reach over 49 °C but can drop rapidly after a storm. Most of the rain falls in the months from July to September in heavy downpours that quickly dry up. The plants and animals found in this desert are uniquely suited to these extreme conditions.

Desert bee

Sonoran desert bees burrow into the ground or use hollow plant stems to create nests. They feed on pollen and nectar from flowering plants. Some of the pollen sticks to their fur and this pollinates (or fertilises) the other flowers they visit. Most desert bees live solitary lives – they don't live in colonies.

Jackrabbit

The jackrabbit's long ears listen for enemies, but they have another use as well – they help to release heat from its body and so keep it cool. Like many other desert animals, jackrabbits are nocturnal. They come out of their burrows at night when temperatures are cooler to feed on desert plants. Bald eagles, burrowing owls, coyotes and mountain lions are their main predators.

Mexican red-kneed tarantula

The hairy red-kneed tarantula digs a burrow in the desert with its strong legs. It has no use for a web and instead uses its hairs to detect passing prey by picking up their vibrations in the air. A lizard or a mouse would make a tasty late-night meal for this tarantula.

Pipevine swallowtail

This beautiful dark blue butterfly has poisonous caterpillars! Why? Butterflies lay their eggs on plants that will provide food for their caterpillars. The leaves of the pipevine contain poisons that are absorbed by the caterpillars as a deterrent to predators who might want to eat them. This greatly increases their chance of survival.

Turkey vulture

This black-feathered bird, with a white beak and bald red head is a turkey vulture. A supreme scavenger, it uses its keen sense of smell to seek out freshly-dead animals. It does not attack living prey. For this reason, it plays an important role in cleaning up the desert!

Gila monster

Camouflaged to blend into the desert landscape, the Gila monster hunts by taste and smell, using its tongue to locate prey. When the Gila monster bites, deadly venom is released into the wound. Frogs, rodents, birds and birds' eggs form its main diet. By storing fat in its tail, it only needs to eat three or four meals a year!

Road runner

These birds can outrun people and kill rattlesnakes! They run on their long legs, head-down with their necks parallel to the ground, using their tails for balance. By running instead of flying, they conserve precious energy. Thriving in the desert of the southwest, road runners hunt small mammals, lizards and other birds.

Sonoran sidewinder

By moving and looping in a sideways direction, the sidewinder rattlesnake tries to make as little contact with the hot sand as possible. The light colouring and pattern provides perfect camouflage as it preys on birds and lizards by injecting them with venom.

Gila woodpecker

Eating mainly insects but also seasonal berries and cactus fruits, the Gila woodpecker is a common resident of the Sonoran Desert. This woodpecker will use its beak to dig out a nest inside the saguaro cactus in which to raise its young in safety. It is preyed upon by carnivores including hawks, bobcats and snakes.

WANT TO KNOW MORE?

Scientists define a desert as being a place where there is less than 25 cm of rainfall per year. Even if it rains in the desert, the heat of the sun can evaporate the rain as soon as it touches the ground. At night, however, the desert can be cold and this creates enough moisture, in the form of mist and fog, for plants and animals to survive.

Central and South America

South America is joined to the North American continent by Central America. This huge landmass is one of the most biodiverse regions in the world, with a wonderful variety of animals living in mountains, remote rainforests, grasslands and deserts. As well as animals, people live here, too, many in cities near the coast.

Climate

This region rests largely within the tropics and has a warm tropical climate, though the high mountains of the Andes are icy cold and the southern tip of the archipelago of Tierra del Fuego is closer to Antarctica. The Andean condor, soaring on mountain thermals, can survey it all.

Rainforests

South America has the world's largest rainforest – it spreads over land in eight countries. In remote areas of the rainforest, new species of plants and animals are discovered almost every day. Over 300 different butterfly species have already been found here.

Grasslands and deserts

In the south, where it is drier, there are grasslands such as the pampas of Argentina and the Atacama Desert – the driest desert in the world. Few animals can survive in the Atacama, though this scorpion is one of them.

Mountains

The Andes, with many peaks over 6,000 m high, is the world's longest mountain chain. It runs all the way down the length of South America on the western side of the continent. Some of the highest peaks are permanently covered in glacial ice and snow. Here, the chinchilla's thick coat protects it from the cold weather.

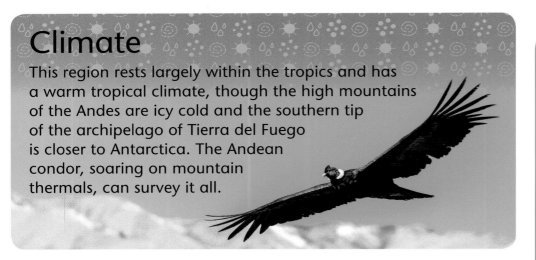

34

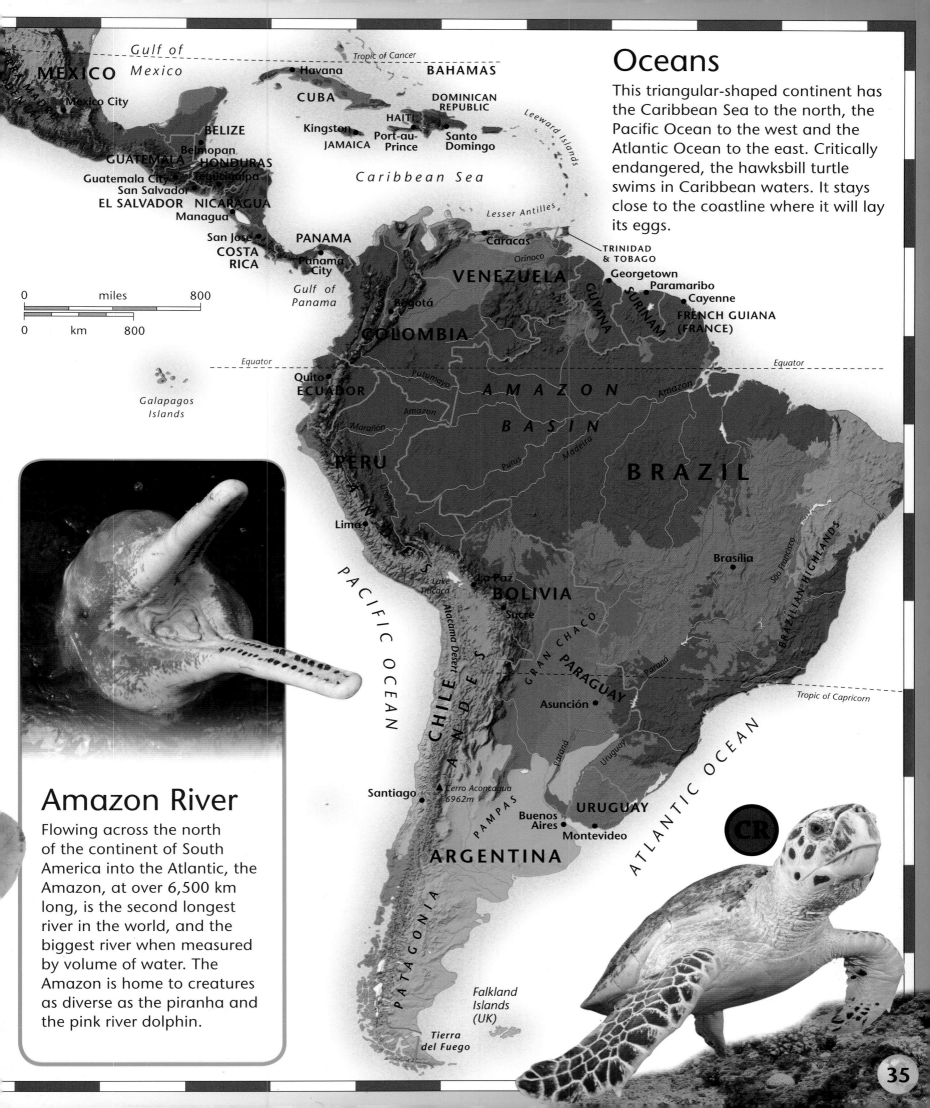

Oceans

This triangular-shaped continent has the Caribbean Sea to the north, the Pacific Ocean to the west and the Atlantic Ocean to the east. Critically endangered, the hawksbill turtle swims in Caribbean waters. It stays close to the coastline where it will lay its eggs.

Map labels

Gulf of Mexico
MEXICO
Mexico City
Tropic of Cancer
Havana
BAHAMAS
CUBA
DOMINICAN REPUBLIC
HAITI
BELIZE
Kingston
Port-au-Prince
Santo Domingo
Belmopan
JAMAICA
Leeward Islands
GUATEMALA
HONDURAS
Guatemala City
Tegucigalpa
San Salvador
EL SALVADOR NICARAGUA
Managua
Caribbean Sea
San Jose
PANAMA
Lesser Antilles
COSTA RICA
Caracas
TRINIDAD & TOBAGO
Panama City
Orinoco
Georgetown
Paramaribo
Gulf of Panama
VENEZUELA
GUYANA
SURINAM
Cayenne
Bogotá
FRENCH GUIANA (FRANCE)
COLOMBIA
Quito
Putumayo
AMAZON
Amazon
Equator
Equator
ECUADOR
Amazon
BASIN
Marañón
Galapagos Islands
PERU
Purus
Madeira
BRAZIL
Lima
Brasília
La Paz
São Francisco
Lake Titicaca
BOLIVIA
BRAZILIAN HIGHLANDS
PACIFIC OCEAN
Sucre
Atacama Desert
GRAN CHACO
PARAGUAY
Paraná
Tropic of Capricorn
ANDES
Asunción
CHILE
Cerro Aconcagua 6962m
Uruguay
Santiago
URUGUAY
PAMPAS
Buenos Aires
Montevideo
ATLANTIC OCEAN
Paraná
PATAGONIA
ARGENTINA
CR
Falkland Islands (UK)
Tierra del Fuego

scale

0 miles 800
0 km 800

Amazon River

Flowing across the north of the continent of South America into the Atlantic, the Amazon, at over 6,500 km long, is the second longest river in the world, and the biggest river when measured by volume of water. The Amazon is home to creatures as diverse as the piranha and the pink river dolphin.

Habitat Focus:
Amazon Rainforest

The largest tropical rainforest in the world, the Amazon rainforest is home to more plant and animal species than any other habitat on Earth. The climate here is wet, warm and humid all year round. Most of the animals of the rainforest are adapted to living in the 'canopy': a maze of vines, branches and leaves high up in the tops of the trees.

Scarlet macaw

This red, yellow and blue bird is called the scarlet macaw. It is the national bird of Honduras. With its hooked beak, perfectly adapted for cracking nuts and seeds, the scarlet macaw is often seen flying above the rainforest canopy. Sadly, these birds are hunted for sale as pets.

Toucan

Living in the canopy, the toucan is easily recognised by its enormous beak, which it uses to reach out for the fruit, insects and eggs that it likes to eat. This noisy bird lives in a small flock. Its body is short and its wings small because it doesn't need to fly great distances.

Poison dart frog

Tropical frogs live in trees to avoid predators on the forest floor. The poison dart frog, however, has another survival strategy – its skin secretes a deadly poison. Traditionally, Amazonian tribespeople used this poison to coat their hunting arrows. On the skin of one dart frog there is enough poison to kill 10 large animals.

Anaconda

The anaconda is the largest snake on Earth and grows up to 10 m long. It is not a venomous snake – it kills its prey by squeezing them until they are dead, then it swallows them whole! Jaguars, deer and crocodiles are not too big to be swallowed by this huge reptile.

Giant anteater

The anteater's long snout and sticky tongue are useful for sniffing out and scooping up its favourite food: ants and termites. A thick fur coat protects the anteater from their bites and stings. Its sharp claws are useful, too, for defence against its main predator, the jaguar.

Harpy eagle

A top predator, the harpy eagle is one of the largest of the eagle species. It preys on the tree-dwelling mammals you are reading about on this page! Harpy eagles mate for life. They build a large nest high up in the canopy, which they will use for many years, as they raise just one chick at a time.

WANT TO KNOW MORE?

Deforestation to make way for crops, cattle and industry is destroying the rainforest habitat and its animals. Local forest tribespeople have also been displaced. Some scientists predict that in 20 years' time half of the rainforest will be lost.

Sloth

Related to the anteater, the sloth is an extremely slow-moving creature. A sloth will sleep for 18 hours a day and stay in the same tree for years. Its diet is to blame for this lack of energy – the leaves that it eats can take up to a month to digest! Its main predators are the jaguar and the harpy eagle.

Jaguar

One of the most dangerous predators in the rainforest, the jaguar can run, swim and climb trees in pursuit of its prey. This big cat can reach almost 2 m long and weigh around 115 kg. The jaguar lives and hunts alone. It preys on large mammals such as deer and capybaras.

Capybara

A relative of the guinea pig, the capybara, at 64 cm tall, is the largest rodent in the world. It lives in the rainforest close to rivers or lakes where it feeds on grasses and water plants. The water is not only a source of food but it also provides the capybara with a quick means of escape from hungry eagles, jaguars and anacondas.

Golden lion tamarin

This rare primate is endangered due to the cutting down of rainforest trees. There are only about 1,500 left in the wild, where they live in family groups. Males help to look after the young, often carrying them on their backs. Tamarins sleep in holes in trees and eat fruit, insects and lizards.

Habitat Focus:
Galápagos Islands

To the west of Ecuador, the Galápagos Islands are home to many unique species including giant turtles and marine iguanas. The British naturalist Charles Darwin visited the islands in 1835 and the animals he saw there inspired his theory of evolution. He realised that the slight variations he observed between the animals from the mainland and from these islands was the result of their adaptation to the environment.

Galápagos giant tortoise

(VU)

This is the largest tortoise in the world, after which the Galápagos Islands were named by Spanish explorers – 'galápago' means 'tortoise' in Spanish. The tortoises on different islands have different shells. Now protected, hunting for their shells and meat in the past has reduced their numbers.

Darwin's finch

There are about 15 species of finch on the Galápagos Islands. Each one varies in size and has a differently-shaped beak, depending on its diet. The small ground finch has a small sharp beak for eating tiny seeds but the large ground finch has a large strong beak for crushing bigger seeds.

Marine iguana

The marine iguana may look fierce but it is in fact a harmless herbivore that feeds on seaweed and algae, which it scrapes off rocks with its sharp teeth. Its colour and size vary from one island to another. Predators such as dogs and rats steal their eggs and young, making the marine iguana vulnerable.

(VU)

Blue-footed booby

This strange-looking bird called the booby walks clumsily on land with its large blue feet, though it can dive expertly from rocks into the sea to catch sardines and anchovies. The male is proud of his blue feet and will wave them around in a mating dance. Red-footed boobies have red feet!

WANT TO KNOW MORE?

The Galápagos Islands are formed from lava that erupted in the sea about a million years ago. There are 19 islands, each with its own particular flora and fauna. Because of its unique ecosystems, this group of islands is protected as a Natural World Heritage Site.

Flightless cormorant

Everywhere else in the world, cormorants can fly but here in the Galápagos they don't need to because they have no major predators. Instead of flying to find food, this cormorant swims underwater in search of eels, squid and fish. Flying cormorants are now extinct in the Galápagos.

VU

Galápagos fur seal

This fur seal lives only in the Galápagos Islands – it does not migrate. In the past it was hunted for its skin and oil, but is now a protected species. It uses its long front flippers to move about on land, where it spends much of its time. A female will give birth to one pup per year.

EN

Lava lizard

Differing in colour from one island to another, the lava lizard uses camouflage as a defence from predators. Colours vary depending on whether they inhabit lava rock or sand. When one male challenges another, it will do 'push ups' to make it appear bigger than its rival. The lava lizard eats beetles, spiders and insects.

Sally lightfoot crab

The rainbow-coloured Sally lightfoot crab has a symbiotic relationship with the Galápagos marine iguana – it is often seen cleaning ticks from the iguana's skin! As well as eating ticks, it feeds on algae found on rocks. 'Lightfoot' is an apt name for this crab because it is a quick-mover and hard to catch.

Galápagos penguin

EN

This penguin, one of the smallest in the world, is endangered because it has many predators on land and in the sea, including snakes, hawks, sharks and sea lions. It eats fish, mainly sardines that it finds close to the shore, but when the weather is poor this can change the sea currents and affect food supply.

Africa

The African continent is the second largest in the world. It is home to 1 billion people and some of the world's most amazing animals, including the biggest and tallest land mammals, over 2,600 species of birds, over 60 species of monkeys, and many endangered animals too. Habitats range from hot, dry deserts to tropical rainforests, high volcanic mountains, flat plains and savannahs.

Climate

Areas near the equator are the hottest and wettest. To the north and south, the climate is more seasonal and there are 'wet' and 'dry' seasons. Rainfall, however, is unpredictable – there can be extreme drought or extreme flood. This can make life hard for both people and animals.

Rainforests

Tropical rainforests are found in the centre of the continent and on the island of Madagascar. These regions can have over 400 cm of rain per year. Compare this with the desert, where often there is less than 5 cm.

Mountains

Millions of years ago, erupting volcanoes in the east of Africa created the Ethiopian Highlands. Further south, Mount Kilimanjaro, a dormant volcano and the highest mountain in Africa, towers over the savannah.

Deserts

The Sahara, in the north of Africa, is the biggest hot desert in the world. There are deserts in the south too: the Namib and Kalahari deserts. Animals that live in the desert are adapted to survive. The dromedary camel can go without water for many days at a time.

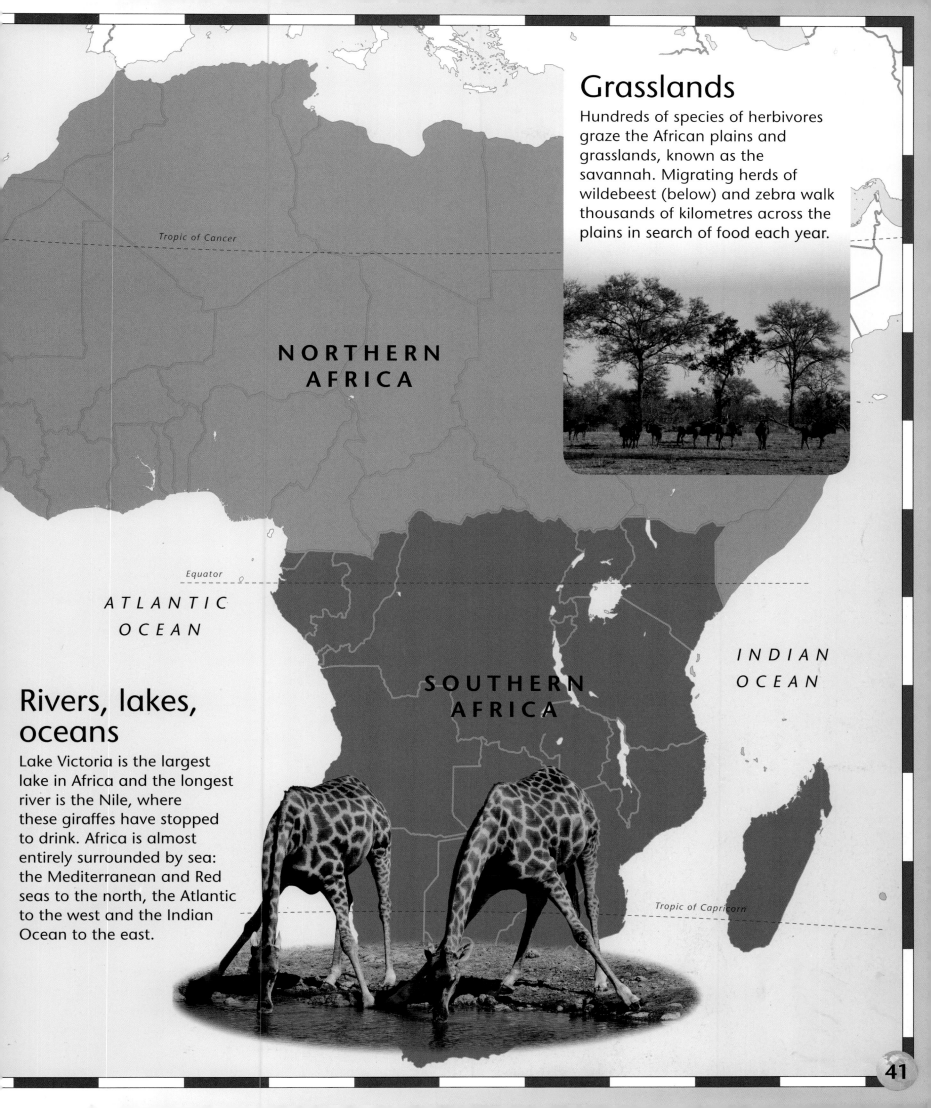

Grasslands

Hundreds of species of herbivores graze the African plains and grasslands, known as the savannah. Migrating herds of wildebeest (below) and zebra walk thousands of kilometres across the plains in search of food each year.

Tropic of Cancer

NORTHERN AFRICA

Equator

ATLANTIC OCEAN

INDIAN OCEAN

SOUTHERN AFRICA

Rivers, lakes, oceans

Lake Victoria is the largest lake in Africa and the longest river is the Nile, where these giraffes have stopped to drink. Africa is almost entirely surrounded by sea: the Mediterranean and Red seas to the north, the Atlantic to the west and the Indian Ocean to the east.

Tropic of Capricorn

Northern Africa

Mediterranean Sea

ATLANTIC OCEAN

Algiers   Tunis

Rabat

MOROCCO   ATLAS MOUNTAINS   **TUNISIA**   Tripoli

Cairo   Suez Canal

Laayoune   **ALGERIA**   **LIBYA**   *LIBYAN DESERT*   **EGYPT**

WESTERN SAHARA   *AHAGGAR*   Red Sea

Tropic of Cancer   Lake Nasser

S A H A R A   D E S E R T

TIBESTI

MAURITANIA

Nouakchott   **MALI**   **NIGER**   **CHAD**

CAPE VERDE   Senegal   *S A H E L*   Khartoum

Praia   **SENEGAL**   Niger   Lake Chad   *Darfur*   **SUDAN**

Dakar   Niamey

GAMBIA   Bamako   Ndjamena   Blue Nile

Banjul   Ouagadougou

Bissau   **BURKINA FASO**   **NIGERIA**   White Nile

GUINEA-BISSAU   **GUINEA**

Conakry   Abuja   **CENTRAL AFRICAN REPUBLIC**   **SOUTH SUDAN**

Freetown   **IVORY COAST**   **GHANA**   **BENIN**   *SUDD*

SIERRA LEONE   **TOGO**   Porto-novo   Juba

Monrovia   Yamoussoukro   **CAMEROON**   Bangui

LIBERIA   Lome

Accra   *Gulf of Guinea*   **DEMOCRATIC REPUBLIC OF CONGO**   **UGANDA**

Yaounde

EQUATORIAL GUINEA   **GABON**   **CONGO**

0   miles   800
0   km   800

For thousands of years, people and animals living in northern Africa have settled along the Nile River or near to the sea because inland it is mostly desert – the Sahara. The animals that live in the desert have to cope not only with a lack of water but also with extreme temperatures, ranging from scorching hot during the day to freezing cold at night. Desert animals have evolved and adapted their behaviour to survive in this harsh environment.

Jerboa

A nocturnal, jumping rodent, the jerboa has long legs that it puts to good use when escaping from predators such as vipers and foxes. It shelters from the desert sun in its underground burrow. The water it needs is provided by its diet of plants, seeds and insects.

Dung beetle

This beetle collects animal faeces (dung), rolls it into a ball and then eats it. Agriculture benefits greatly from the dung beetle because it serves to recycle animal waste and fertilise the soil. The Ancient Egyptians recognised the importance of the dung beetle (or scarab) in their statues and hieroglyphics.

Nile crocodile

When animals stop to drink in the river they are at their most vulnerable from the Nile crocodile. With its huge body (averaging 5 m long) almost entirely submerged, it swims silently towards unsuspecting prey and overpowers them using its strong jaws and sharp teeth.

Ethiopian wolf

In the Ethiopian highlands, there are only about 500 of these endangered wolves remaining in the wild. They hunt alone, looking for small rodents, though they will hunt in a pack for larger prey such as antelope. Males live with one or two females in an extended family group.

Desert horned viper

The little horns above the eyes identify this snake as a horned viper. This deadly snake has hollow, retractable fangs containing enough poison to kill large prey. Vipers don't stalk their prey, instead they bury themselves in the sand and wait for prey (including the fox and the jerboa) to pass by.

TREA

nara

DJIBOUTI

• Djibouti

IIOPIAN
HLANDS

HORN OF
AFRICA

is Ababa

HIOPIA

SOMALIA

INDIAN OCEAN

• Mogadishu

NYA

Deathstalker scorpion

As its name suggests, the deathstalker scorpion is one of the most deadly scorpions in the world. Normally, a scorpion will only sting its victim in self-defence, but because this scorpion has relatively small pincers it will grab its prey then sting it with paralysing venom to ensure it can't escape.

Dromedary camel

This camel's body is adapted to desert life in many ways: long eyelashes keep sand from its eyes; pads on the bottom of its feet protect them from hot sand; it has a hump that stores fat away from the body; a digestive system that recycles water and a cooling system for the brain.

Southern Africa

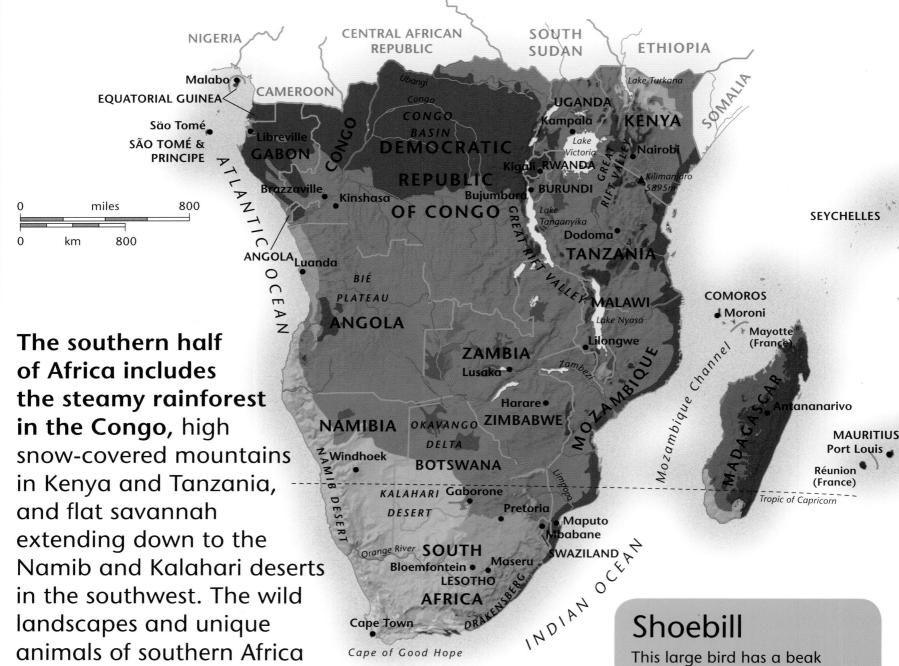

NIGERIA
CENTRAL AFRICAN REPUBLIC
SOUTH SUDAN
ETHIOPIA

Malabo
EQUATORIAL GUINEA
CAMEROON
Ubangi
Congo
Lake Turkana
SOMALIA

São Tomé
SÃO TOMÉ & PRINCIPE
Libreville
GABON
CONGO
CONGO BASIN
DEMOCRATIC REPUBLIC OF CONGO
UGANDA
Kampala
KENYA
Lake Victoria
Nairobi

Brazzaville
Kinshasa
Kigali RWANDA
BURUNDI
Bujumbura
GREAT RIFT VALLEY
Kilimanjaro 5895m

ATLANTIC OCEAN

ANGOLA Luanda
BIÉ PLATEAU
Lake Tanganyika
Dodoma
TANZANIA

miles 800
km 800

SEYCHELLES

ANGOLA
ZAMBIA
Lusaka
MALAWI
Lake Nyasa
Lilongwe
Zambezi

COMOROS
Moroni
Mayotte (France)

Mozambique Channel

ZIMBABWE
Harare
MOZAMBIQUE
MADAGASCAR
Antananarivo

NAMIBIA
OKAVANGO DELTA

MAURITIUS
Port Louis
Réunion (France)

NAMIB DESERT
Windhoek
BOTSWANA

Tropic of Capricorn

KALAHARI DESERT
Gaborone
Pretoria
Maputo
Mbabane
SWAZILAND

Orange River
SOUTH AFRICA
Bloemfontein
Maseru
LESOTHO
DRAKENSBERG

Limpopo

INDIAN OCEAN

Cape Town
Cape of Good Hope

The southern half of Africa includes the steamy rainforest in the Congo, high snow-covered mountains in Kenya and Tanzania, and flat savannah extending down to the Namib and Kalahari deserts in the southwest. The wild landscapes and unique animals of southern Africa attract tourists to the Maasai Mara, Serengeti and Kruger National Parks.

Shoebill

This large bird has a beak that can grow to 24 cm long! It stands alone in the muddy waters of the swamp, hoping to catch a lungfish, frog or watersnake for its meal. Adult birds have blue-grey feathers. They flap and glide over short distances like pelicans.

Panther chameleon

By changing its colour, a chameleon can signal its mood, defend its territory or find a mate. It has other adaptations, useful for catching flying insects – eyes that can move separately to look in two different directions at once and a long, sticky tongue. Its tail is also useful for balancing on thin branches.

Fruit bat

Sometimes called a 'flying fox', the fruit bat feeds on fruit, flowers, nectar and pollen that it finds using its large eyes and excellent sense of smell. It feeds mostly at night and during the day rests hanging upside down in a tree, with its leathery wings wrapped around its body.

Pangolin VU

The pangolin's scales are like body armour, protecting it from predators while it raids ant and termite nests. When it feels threatened it will curl up into ball and tuck its head and feet out of sight. Pangolins were once hunted by humans because they were believed to be magical creatures.

Chimpanzee

In the rainforest in the Congo, these intelligent animals use stones to crack open nuts, and long twigs to scoop out termites from nests. Chimpanzees can walk upright when carrying objects. They are social animals – they can laugh and show a variety of emotions.

Mountain gorilla CR

Living in a mountain habitat in East Africa, there are only around 720 of these magnificent gorillas left in the world. The temperature in the mountains can fall to freezing at night, so their thick fur provides warmth. Gorillas are vegetarian; they eat forest plants, roots and berries. The silverback male, twice as big as the female, protects the family group.

WANT TO KNOW MORE?

Madagascar was once joined to the mainland but millions of years ago it split from Africa to form a separate island. This separation resulted in the gradual evolution of new animal species on the island. For example, only in Madagascar will you find panther chameleons and lemurs.

Habitat Focus:
African Savannah

Herds of wildebeest, impala and elephants follow ancient pathways across the African savannah grasslands, as their ancestors have done for thousands of years. They will follow the seasonal rainfall that brings fresh green grass and water to the sun-baked dry pastures.

African elephant **(VU)**

The largest land animal on Earth, the African elephant eats a diet of grasses, twigs, roots and fruit, and drinks up to 227 litres of water a day! Those enormous ears act like fans to cool its body. With its long trunk it can smell and grasp things, as well as suck up water and shower itself!

Lion

It is the job of the female lion to feed her family. The male lion is too big and conspicuous for the hunt so stays behind to look after the cubs and defend their territory from hyenas or other lions. A group of females will stalk and then ambush weak or young wildebeest, zebra or giraffe as a meal for the pride.

Wildebeest (or gnu)

Herds of noisy wildebeest migrate huge distances every year across East Africa and the south in search of new pastures. On the way, they may have to cross wild rivers and not all of them will survive the journey. Lions, cheetahs and hyenas wait to prey on those that are too old or weak to keep up with the herd.

Hippopotamus

The eyes and ears of the hippopotamus remain alert to danger as it rests in the river. Its webbed toes act like paddles in the water, where it stays for most of the day to avoid the heat of the sun. When threatened, it can move quickly and will not hesitate to use its sharp tusks. Later in the day, it will move with its herd to graze on the savannah.

Giraffe

The tallest land animal on Earth is the giraffe. It uses its height to scan the landscape for predators, especially lions, and also to pick out the juiciest leaves from the topmost branches. Because the giraffe is so tall, its heart has to work much harder than the human heart to pump blood around its body and up to its brain.

Spotted hyena

A noisy predator, the spotted hyena lives in a group (known as a clan) to hunt, raise its young and defend its territory. Hyenas are not just scavengers (living on dead meat) but skilful hunters too. They will work together to bring down larger prey, such as antelope, by chasing them to the point of exhaustion.

Zebra

Zebras migrate alongside wildebeest because they know there is safety in numbers. The zebra's striped coat acts as camouflage to break up its body outline. Sadly, however, it is the attractiveness of their coat that makes them a target for hunters and poachers.

Rhinoceros

There are two species of rhinoceros in Africa: the black and the white. Both are endangered due to hunting for their horns. They may look fierce, but they are plant-eaters and will only attack to defend their young or their territory.

EN

WANT TO KNOW MORE?

Carnivores such as lions and hyenas have sharp canine teeth for tearing meat. Herbivores such as elephants and hippos have strong, flat molars for grinding tough plants and roots, and tusks that they use for defence.

Asia

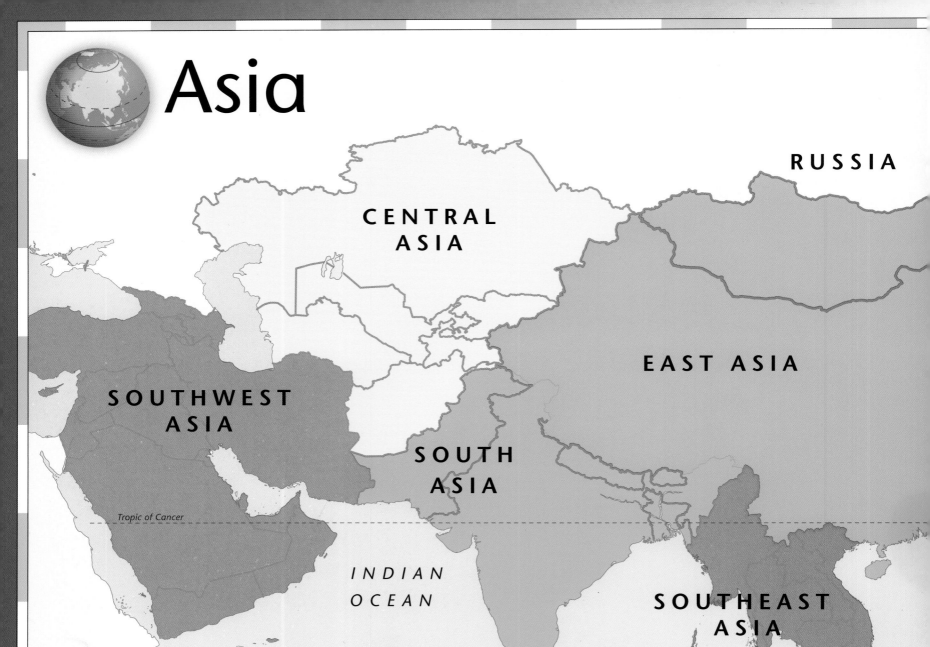

RUSSIA

CENTRAL ASIA

EAST ASIA

SOUTHWEST ASIA

SOUTH ASIA

Tropic of Cancer

INDIAN OCEAN

SOUTHEAST ASIA

Equator

The largest continent on Earth, Asia stretches from Russia in the north to Indonesia in the south. Over 4 billion people live here. Asia has some of the most densely populated cities in the world including Tokyo in Japan and Mumbai in India, as well as wilderness areas in Mongolia where few people live. There are flat frozen landscapes in the north, dry deserts and high snow-covered mountains in central Asia, while tropical rainforests cover much of the south.

Climate

Temperatures in the south of the continent are hot, but towards Siberia in the north it is extremely cold. Across much of central Asia the climate is dry, but in the southeast it is wet, especially during the summer, because of heavy monsoon rainfall.

Deserts

In Asia, there are both hot and cold deserts. A hot desert region stretches from the Arabian Desert in Saudi Arabia, through Iran and Pakistan, to the cold Gobi Desert in Mongolia. Here a Bactrian camel is the best form of transport.

Grasslands

An area of grassland known as the steppes stretches across the Asian continent from Russia to Mongolia. It is home to a variety of rare animals including saiga antelope and snow leopards.

Mountains

On the border of China and Nepal, Mount Everest in the Himalaya is the world's highest mountain at 8,848 m. Nothing can live permanently on Everest because there is not enough oxygen but wild yaks can graze on the lower slopes.

PACIFIC
OCEAN

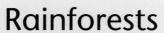

Equator

Rainforests

The rainforests of southern Asia are among the oldest rainforests on Earth. They are home to thousands of different species of flowering plants, trees and forest animals, including the endangered Borneo orangutan and the Sumatran tiger.

Oceans

The Asian continent is bordered in the west by the Red Sea and the Mediterranean, and in the east by the Pacific. To the north are the cooler Arctic waters, while to the south, the tropical Indian Ocean is teeming with brightly-coloured fish, including this clown triggerfish (above).

Southwest Asia

This landscape of southwest Asia is mainly deep desert sand, mountain and scrub. The animals living here have learned to survive with little water. Rainfall is highest in the mountain regions in Iran, where dense forests are home to bears and wolves. Not so long ago, lions, leopards and cheetahs lived here, but now they are rare in the wild – though you may still see them in national parks such as the Kavir National Park in Iran.

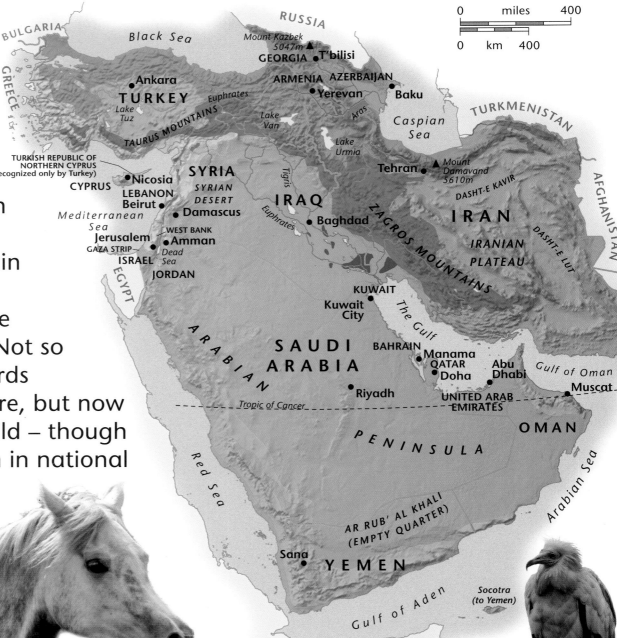

0 miles 400

0 km 400

BULGARIA
Black Sea
RUSSIA
Mount Kazbek 5047m ▲
GEORGIA • T'bilisi
GREECE
Ankara •
TURKEY
ARMENIA
• Yerevan
AZERBAIJAN
• Baku
TURKMENISTAN
Euphrates
Lake Tuz
Lake Van
Aras
Caspian Sea
TAURUS MOUNTAINS
Lake Urmia
Tehran •
▲ Mount Damavand 5610m
DASHT-E KAVIR
AFGHANISTAN
TURKISH REPUBLIC OF NORTHERN CYPRUS (recognized only by Turkey)
CYPRUS • Nicosia
SYRIA
SYRIAN DESERT
Tigris
IRAN
IRANIAN PLATEAU
DASHT-E LUT
LEBANON
Beirut •
• Damascus
IRAQ
• Baghdad
ZAGROS MOUNTAINS
Mediterranean Sea
Euphrates
Jerusalem •
WEST BANK
• Amman
GAZA STRIP
Dead Sea
ISRAEL
JORDAN
EGYPT
KUWAIT
Kuwait City •
The Gulf
SAUDI ARABIA
BAHRAIN
Manama •
QATAR
Abu Dhabi •
Gulf of Oman
Muscat •
A R A B I A N
• Riyadh
• Doha
UNITED ARAB EMIRATES
Tropic of Cancer
OMAN
P E N I N S U L A
Red Sea
Arabian Sea
AR RUB' AL KHALI (EMPTY QUARTER)
Sana •
Y E M E N
Gulf of Aden
Socotra (to Yemen)

Arabian horse

Many domestic horses have been bred from the handsome Arabian horse because of its good nature, speed and strength. The wedge head-shape and high tail are distinguishing features. This was the favoured horse of the nomadic Bedouin people. Nowadays, it is one of the most popular horse breeds all over the world.

Egyptian vulture

EN

This small vulture, sometimes called 'pharaoh's chicken', feeds mainly on carrion (dead meat) and other bird's eggs. Egyptian vultures use stones to crack open larger eggs – this clever use of a 'tool' is unusual behaviour for a bird. They are endangered due to hunting.

Syrian hamster (VU)

Popular as a pet but now vulnerable in the wild, this hamster can live in deserts, grasslands and mountains. It digs a burrow in the earth and builds a nest to sleep in. At night, it goes out in search of food: mainly seeds and leaves.

Caracal

Widespread in mountainous regions in southwest Asia, the caracal is recognised by the long tufts of hair on the tips of its ears. This long-legged cat is known for its ability to leap up in the air to catch birds. Young kittens will stay with their mother for up to a year to learn how to hunt and survive.

Arabian oryx (VU)

This oryx was once extinct in the wild but was rescued by zoos and reintroduced into its native desert habitat in 1980. It has a distinctive white coat with brown legs and black stripes around the neck and down the nose. Both males and females have long horns. It grazes over a wide area on grasses, roots, fruits and trees.

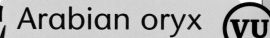

Persian leaf-nosed bat

One of the smallest bats on the Asian continent, the leaf-nosed bat is only 78 mm in length. It has large ears and a large nose, shaped like a leaf, which it uses to echo locate prey. When it calls out, it listens to the returning echoes to identify and locate nearby obstacles or a passing insect meal.

Nubian ibex (VU)

A wild goat, this male Nubian ibex has long, backward curving horns that can grow up to a metre in length. The females have much smaller horns. This ibex lives in dry mountainous areas, feeding on grasses and leaves, in large herds of only males or females. It is a vulnerable species due to hunting in the past.

WANT TO KNOW MORE?

Conservationists are trying to save two critically endangered cats from extinction: the Arabian leopard, of which there are fewer than 250 left, and the Asiatic cheetah, which is now found only in Iran.

CR

Baboon

Hamadryas baboons live in the southwestern tip of the Yemen, where they feed on fruit, roots, insects and small mammals. Twice as big as the brown-coloured female, the male has a cape of silver fur. Baboons are social animals – they enjoy the company of others, and live in family groups.

Central Asia

Far from the open ocean, central Asia has dusty deserts, high mountains and extensive grasslands, known as steppes. In summer, the land bakes in the sun, but in winter it is blanketed in a thick covering of snow. In Kazakhstan there are flat, fertile plains cultivated with food crops such as wheat and barley.

RUSSIA

RUSSIA

Tobol

Ishim

Irtysh

Astana

Ural

CASPIAN DEPRESSION

KIRGHIZ STEPPE

SARYARQA UPLANDS

KAZAKHSTAN

Lake Balkhash

Lake Alakol

USTYURT PLATEAU

Aral Sea

Syr Dar'ya

Caspian Sea

KYZYL KUM DESERT

Bishkek

Ozero Issyk-Kul

Pobeda Pe 7439m

KYRGYZSTAN

TIEN SHAN

TURAN LOWLANDS

UZBEKISTAN

Tashkent

CHINA

KARA KUM DESERT

TURKMENISTAN

Amu Dar'ya

TAJIKISTAN

Pik Ismail Samani 7495m

PAMIRS

Ashgabat

Dushanbe

Pamir

IRAN

HINDU KUSH

Kabul

AFGHANISTAN

PAKISTAN

Helmand

| 0 | miles | 400 |
| 0 | km | 400 |

CR Saiga antelope

This antelope is critically endangered. Once its habitat stretched across the steppes from Russia to Mongolia, but now it is found only in Kazakhstan due to hunting for its horns, which only the males have. Notice its unusually long nose – used for filtering out dust!

VU Marbled polecat

Marking its territory with scent, this polecat is a small but skilful predator of rabbits, birds, lizards and frogs. Found in grassland habitats across this region, it is recognisable by its long body, marbled coat and bushy tail. It has small but sharp teeth.

Peregrine falcon

The world's fastest bird, the peregrine falcon can bring down other birds in mid-air using its sharp talons. It makes its nest on mountains or cliffs and sometimes even in cities on high window ledges. It will spend the winter in northwest India.

The mountains and steppes of Kazakhstan have long been a breeding ground for falcons and golden eagles. Hunting with eagles is an ancient tradition for the Kazakhs. Today, the eagle-hunter's skills are being used to protect Kazakhstan's eagle population.

Bobak marmot

It may look like an overfed North American prairie dog, but it's not – this is a bobak marmot. It weighs around 5 kg – males are slightly larger than females. Bobaks feed on grasses and vegetable crops from the edge of cultivated fields. They live together in large families.

Snow leopard

Living in remote mountain areas in Central Asia and the Himalaya, the snow leopard has a pale coat to camouflage against the winter snow. Balancing on its wide paws, it leaps over bare rock in pursuit of prey, mainly wild sheep, antelope and markhor. There are only around 6,000 left in the wild due to hunting and habitat loss.

Corsac fox

Found in semi-desert and steppe regions, the Corsac fox feeds on rodents, birds, insects and fruit. Its thick silver-grey fur provides protection from the cold winters and camouflage from predators such as eastern imperial eagles.

Chukar partridge

This bird gets its name from its loud repeated 'chuck' call. Widespread across Asia on rocky hillsides and scrubland, it is also recognisable by the distinctive black and white bands on its head and sides. It eats seeds and insects.

South Asia

The highest mountains in the world, the Himalaya, separate south Asia from the rest of the Asian continent. This mountain barrier has allowed unique animal species to evolve in the region and has also determined the weather locally. A warm, wet climate has produced tropical forests over much of India. In the centre and south, the Deccan Plateau is an area of fertile land where many people live and grow crops.

AFGHANISTAN

HINDU KUSH

KARAKORAM RANGE

K2 8611m

Islamabad

PAKISTAN

IRAN

Indus

Indus

HIMALAYA

CHINA

New Delhi

THAR DESERT

NEPAL

Mt Everest 8848m

Kathmandu

BHUTAN

Thimphu

Yamuna

Ganges

Ghaghara

Ganges

BANGLADESH

Dhaka

Brahmaputra

BURMA

VINDHYA RANGE

Tropic of Cancer

Narmada

INDIA

Mouths of the Ganges

Arabian Sea

DECCAN PLATEAU

Godavari

Bay of Bengal

WESTERN GHATS

Krishna

Andaman Islands (to India)

Laccadive Islands

Nicobar Islands (to India)

SRI LANKA

Colombo

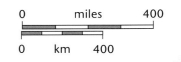

0   miles   400

0   km   400

Bengal tiger

The biggest of all the cats, the Bengal tiger is a terrifying predator. The black stripes break up the outline of its body so that it can stalk prey closely without being seen. With its powerful body and huge bite, it can bring down animals as large as buffalo. This tiger has excellent night vision and a keen sense of smell and hearing.

Great Indian hornbill

This magnificent bird eats mainly fruit, especially figs, but occasionally small mammals, lizards and birds that it catches in its massive curved beak. Hornbills nest in holes in trees. When the young hatch, the parents seal them inside the nest to protect them.

King cobra

The largest venomous snake in the world, the king cobra can grow up to 5.5 m long. When this cobra rears up, it is ready to strike. Its hollow fangs are like hypodermic needles from which it can squirt poison. This snake has a limited diet – it eats only other snakes.

Peacock

The male peacock shows off his beautiful feathers in an attempt to attract a mate. He has to do his best because the female peahen, which has much duller colours, chooses the most eye-catching display. Wild peacocks live in forests.

Markhor

The national animal of Pakistan, the markhor is a wild goat with corkscrew horns that the males use in the mating season to fight each other. Markhors are adapted to their life in the mountains. For example, their coat is short in summer but grows thicker in winter.

Water buffalo

In the wild, the water buffalo spends much of its time in water, cooling off and avoiding insects. Domesticated buffalo are used to plough fields and provide milk. Their huge horns can measure up to 2 m long.

Indian rhinoceros

Thick protective skin hangs in folds like body armour on the Indian rhinoceros. Layers of baked mud act as sunblock and stop the biting insects too! Rhinos have a keen sense of smell and hearing, though their eyesight is poor – that's why they tend to panic and charge when startled by a noise.

Mynah bird

A noisy bird, the common mynah is a natural mimic. In the wild, it communicates by learning the whistles, calls and songs of other mynahs in its locality. Mynahs make popular pets because they can copy the sound of the human voice.

Asian elephant

Like the water buffalo, the Asian elephant has been trained as a working animal, mainly for moving heavy objects such as logs. It feeds on grass and leaves that it pulls up with its trunk. Its body and ears are smaller than those of the African elephant.

Eastern Asia

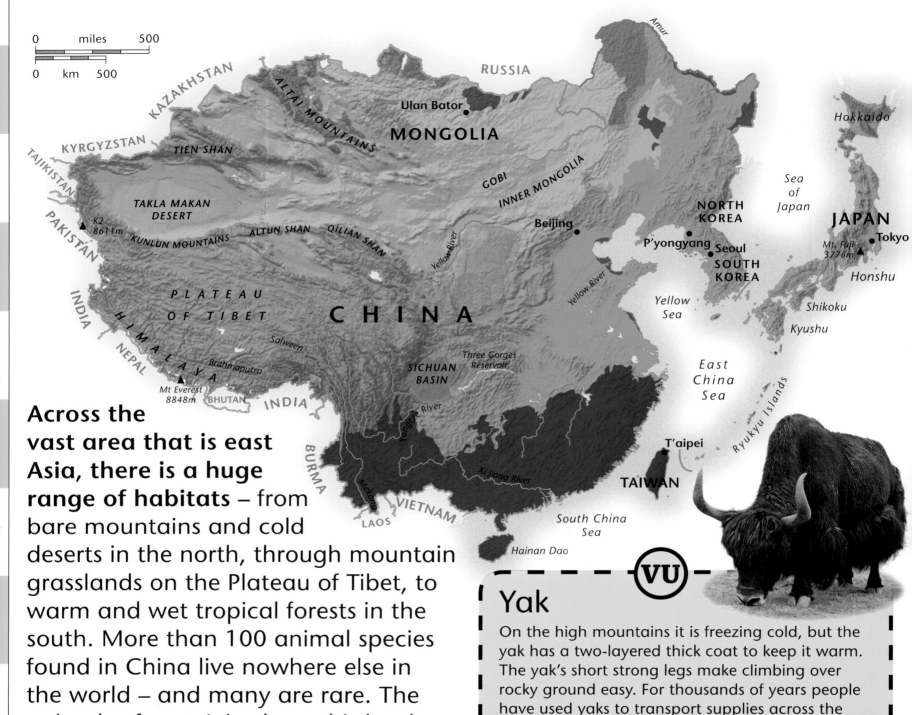

Across the vast area that is east Asia, there is a huge range of habitats – from bare mountains and cold deserts in the north, through mountain grasslands on the Plateau of Tibet, to warm and wet tropical forests in the south. More than 100 animal species found in China live nowhere else in the world – and many are rare. The animals of east Asia share this land with over 1.5 billion people, who live mainly in the east.

Yak

VU

On the high mountains it is freezing cold, but the yak has a two-layered thick coat to keep it warm. The yak's short strong legs make climbing over rocky ground easy. For thousands of years people have used yaks to transport supplies across the mountains, as well as for their meat, milk and hair.

Chinese alligator

CR

Living in freshwater marshes, lakes and ponds off the Yangtze River, the Chinese alligator spends most of the day warming its body in the sun. It is smaller but has more body armour than the American alligator. Now critically endangered, this alligator is being bred in zoos and reintroduced into protected wild habitats.

Golden snub-nosed monkey

EN

Found only in the mountain forests of central China, the golden snub-nosed monkey is so-called because of its golden fur and tiny nose. These monkeys eat mainly lichens but also flowers and fruits. They are preyed on by goshawks, leopards, tigers and golden eagles.

EN

Red-crowned crane

EN

The marshes and riverbanks of eastern China and Japan are the feeding grounds of the elegant red-crowned crane. These cranes are omnivores, with a varied diet of fish, rodents, amphibians, reeds and grasses. They are famous for their dance moves – jumping, bowing and wing flapping – especially during courtship.

EN

Przewalski's horse

The wild Przewalski's horse was once extinct in its natural home on the steppes of central Asia and Mongolia but has now been bred in captivity and reintroduced into national parks. Living together in small family groups, these horses have never been tamed – they are truly 'wild'.

Golden pheasant

A symbol of beauty and good luck in China, the golden pheasant is found in mountainous forests where it feeds on leaves and insects. At night, it will roost up in the trees for safety. With a golden head and bright red body, the male is more colourful than the female.

Japanese macaque

Sometimes called 'snow monkeys' because they live in cold areas, these Japanese macaques are keeping warm by bathing in a hot spring. They live in mountain forests in Japan where they feed on a variety of plants and insects, depending on the season. They are preyed on by wild dogs and mountain eagles.

Giant panda

The giant panda is a fussy eater – eating only bamboo shoots – so when the bamboo forests were cleared for farming, pandas had nothing to eat. Now pandas are a rare and protected species. Scientists try to breed them in zoos, but this is not always successful.

EN

Southeast Asia

Mountains and tropical rainforests cover much of southeast Asia. A warm, wet climate dominates this area. The mountains on the islands are actually volcanoes; many of them are still active. Fed by monsoon rainfall, the rainforests are valuable both for timber and wildlife. On island habitats such as Indonesia, rare and exotic species have evolved that are different from those found on the mainland.

Monkey-eating eagle

About the height of an average, 6-year-old child, this is one of the largest and rarest eagles in the world. The flying lemur is its main food, but these eagles also eat squirrels, lizards, fruit bats and snakes.

Slow loris

The slow loris twists slowly around branches, grasping firmly with its hands and feet. It feeds at night on insects, small birds, eggs and fruit. Snakes, orangutans – and humans are its main predators. The slow loris has specially adapted hands so that it can stay in one position for hours.

Orangutan

Native to the rainforests of Sumatra and Borneo, orangutans live in the trees, hardly ever coming to the ground. The destruction of their forest habitats to clear land for farming and housing has led to the orangutan becoming critically endangered.

EN

Malayan tapir

The black and white colouring of the Malayan tapir helps to camouflage its shape. The tapir has an excellent sense of smell and hearing, but poor eyesight. It eats leaves and new shoots found in the forest, feeding mainly at night. It is endangered largely due to loss of its habitat to farming.

Flying lemur

Eating mainly leaves, the flying lemur leaps from tree to tree with its limbs outstretched. Flaps of skin join the limbs to the body, allowing it to glide. It is not strictly a lemur, but more like a squirrel.

WANT TO KNOW MORE?

The island of Sumatra is home to another rare species: the Sumatran rhinoceros, often called the 'hairy rhino'. This rhinoceros has had its horn removed to protect it from poachers who kill rhinos for their horns. Fossils of the Sumatran rhinoceros have been found that can be traced back millions of years.

Praying mantis

Cleverly camouflaged to look like a green leaf, a praying mantis sits in wait for its next meal. It holds its front legs in the air, ready to strike – this is the 'praying pose' from which it is named. The female praying mantis is larger than the male and will sometimes eat the male during mating.

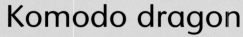

VU

Komodo dragon

The largest lizard in the world, the Komodo dragon uses its forked tongue to taste the air for deer, boar, water buffalo or dead meat. The Komodo dragon attacks its prey with its teeth and claws. When it bites, toxic saliva infects the wound so that even if the prey escapes it will die days later from blood poisoning as the Komodo dragon stalks it to its death.

Habitat Focus:
Pacific Ocean

The largest and deepest ocean on Earth, the Pacific seafloor has a shelf that extends from the coast for about 20–40 km then slopes down steeply before dropping into a deep trench. The Mariana Trench in the western Pacific is 11,000 m deep. Most sea creatures live in the warm shallower waters, but there are some, including the giant octopus, that prefer to live in the cold, darker depths.

Luminous jellyfish

Below 1,000 m the ocean is black because sunlight cannot penetrate that far down. In order to find a mate or to lure prey, some animals make their own light. For example, this jellyfish has luminous body parts that glow in the dark. We call this 'bioluminescence'.

Whale shark

Growing to a length of up to 14 m, the whale shark is the largest fish in the ocean. It feeds on plankton and small fish that swim into its huge open mouth as it moves slowly through the water. Filters in the shark's gills separate the food from the water, then the water passes out through the gills.

Sea cucumber

Crawling along the ocean floor, this sea cucumber may look harmless but if attacked it will release a toxic chemical into the water to stun its attacker. Sea cucumbers are scavengers, feeding on dead matter and plankton.

VU

Humpback whale

You can recognise a humpback whale by its huge front flippers – which it beats like wings. Humpback whales feed in cold waters but breed in warm waters. This humpback whale will migrate along the coast of Japan to summer feeding grounds in the Bering Sea, off the coast of Russia and Alaska.

Pacific manta ray

One of the largest rays in the world, the Pacific manta ray feeds on microscopic plankton, scooping it up as it swims along. Global numbers of mantas are in decline due to overfishing.

Cuttlefish

Hunting fish and crustaceans in shallow water, the cuttlefish uses camouflage to stalk its prey by changing its colour to blend into the background. It moves by propulsion, sucking water in and then squirting it out. When threatened, it will release a cloud of ink to confuse predators while it escapes.

Plankton

Tiny plants (called phytoplankton) or animals (zooplankton) drift through the water just below the surface. Plankton is at the beginning of the ocean food chain. Fish and other water animals eat plankton and bigger fish, sharks and seals eat the plankton eaters.

Giant painted frogfish

The painted frogfish is a master of disguise. It has the ability to change its skin to any colour or texture to match the environment. Notice its big mouth – this carnivore will eat any small animal that passes.

Giant Pacific octopus

Found at depths of 2,000 m in the North Pacific off the coast of Russia and Japan, the giant Pacific octopus feeds on crabs, scallops, lobsters and fish. The suckers on its eight arms are lined with hooks for gripping on to prey. Sperm whales and harbour seals are its main predators.

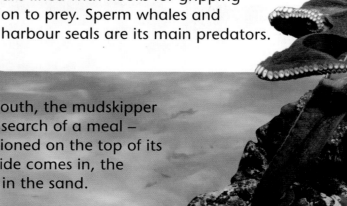

Mudskipper

An amphibious fish that breathes through its skin and the lining of its mouth, the mudskipper can walk across the mud on its fins in search of a meal – a small crab or shellfish. Its eyes, positioned on the top of its head, look out for danger. When the tide comes in, the mudskipper will go back to its burrow in the sand.

Australasia

The biggest country and largest island in this region is Australia. It is so big that it is a continent in its own right. The region also includes New Zealand, Papua New Guinea, Fiji and a number of smaller Pacific islands. Close to 40 million people live here, but as they mostly live near to the sea, there are wilderness areas inland where animals live, almost without any interaction with the human population.

ASIA

PAPUA NEW GUINEA

AUSTRALASIA

AUSTRALIA

TASMANIA

Climate

The Pacific Islands and northern Australia have a tropical climate, but in the interior of Australia it is mainly desert with low rainfall and high temperatures. The climate is cooler in the south-east and in New Zealand.

Mountains

The highest mountains in this region are in Papua New Guinea, where Mount Wilheim reaches 4,509 m high. You can see snow-capped mountains in the Australian Alps and on the North Island of New Zealand there are active volcanoes.

Rainforests

Tropical and subtropical rainforests in Papua New Guinea and in northeast Australia support a rich variety of plant and animal life including this tree kangaroo. Compared to kangaroos that hop on the ground, they have shorter hind legs and claws for climbing trees.

Equator

PACIFIC
OCEAN

SOLOMON
ISLANDS

FIJI

Tropic of Capricorn

Tasman
Sea

NEW
ZEALAND

SOUTHERN
OCEAN

Oceans

The islands of Australasia are surrounded by ocean – the Indian Ocean to the west, the Pacific Ocean to the north and east, and the Southern Ocean to the south. Some dangerous creatutres are found off the coasts including the great white shark and the box jellyfish.

Deserts

Dry, scorching hot deserts cover a large part of Australia. Few people live here, though some Aboriginal people do still live off the land, using survival skills developed over thousands of years. Animals such as dingoes, kangaroos and this thorny devil lizard have also adapted to this harsh environment.

Australia and New Zealand

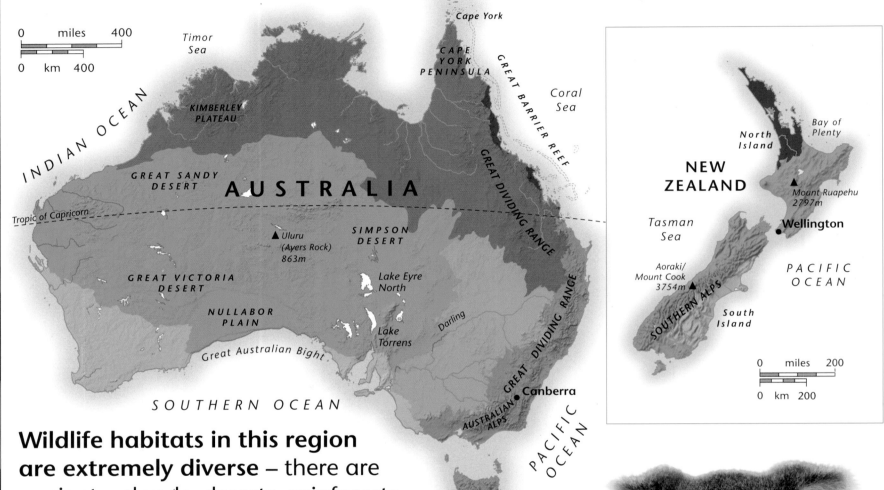

0 miles 400
0 km 400

Timor Sea

INDIAN OCEAN

Cape York

CAPE YORK PENINSULA

GREAT BARRIER REEF

Coral Sea

KIMBERLEY PLATEAU

GREAT SANDY DESERT

A U S T R A L I A

Tropic of Capricorn

▲ *Uluru (Ayers Rock) 863m*

SIMPSON DESERT

GREAT DIVIDING RANGE

GREAT VICTORIA DESERT

Lake Eyre North

NULLABOR PLAIN

Lake Torrens

Darling

Great Australian Bight

SOUTHERN OCEAN

GREAT DIVIDING RANGE

● **Canberra**

AUSTRALIAN ALPS

PACIFIC OCEAN

Tasmania

NEW ZEALAND

North Island

Bay of Plenty

▲ *Mount Ruapehu 2797m*

Tasman Sea

● **Wellington**

Aoraki/ Mount Cook 3754m

SOUTHERN ALPS

South Island

PACIFIC OCEAN

0 miles 200
0 km 200

Wildlife habitats in this region are extremely diverse – there are ancient uplands, deserts, rainforests and grasslands in Australia; and in New Zealand, there are alpine meadows, snow-capped mountains and volcanoes. The interior of Australia is mostly hot, dry desert known as 'the outback' and at its heart is Uluru – a massive 600 million-year-old red rock. The remoteness of these islands means that extraordinary animals such as the platypus and kangaroo are not found in the wild anywhere else in the world.

Koala

Not really a bear, the koala is a marsupial – an animal that raises its young inside a pouch in its body. The koala feeds at night on the leaves of the eucalyptus, using its sharp claws to grip on to the tree bark. Then it sleeps all day!

Sydney funnel-web spider

This is one of the most deadly spiders in the world. The funnel-web spider spins a silky thread to trip up prey and then it bites them with its powerful venom-filled fangs. Sometimes these spiders stray into people's homes, but fortunately there is an antidote to their venom.

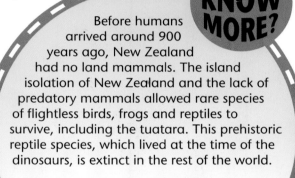

Kiwi

Living in the forests of New Zealand, the shy kiwi comes out to feed after dark. Unusually for a bird, it has nostrils on the tip of its long pointed beak. This helps it to find food, mainly earthworms, insects and frogs. A kiwi's wings are tiny – they don't need to be any bigger because it can't fly.

Tasmanian devil

Living only in Tasmania, the Tasmanian devil looks like a fierce black dog. It feeds on dead animals, particularly birds, wombats and sheep. It is a marsupial, with a pouch in which it suckles and protects its babies (or 'joeys') as they grow. They are preyed on by eagles and masked owls.

Duck-billed platypus

Perfectly adapted to life in rivers and streams, the duck-billed platypus has webbed feet and a streamlined body for swimming, a flat tail for balance and for storing fat, and a bendy beak for searching out food. The platypus doesn't have teeth inside its mouth; instead it has ridges for crushing prey such as crabs.

WANT TO KNOW MORE?

Before humans arrived around 900 years ago, New Zealand had no land mammals. The island isolation of New Zealand and the lack of predatory mammals allowed rare species of flightless birds, frogs and reptiles to survive, including the tuatara. This prehistoric reptile species, which lived at the time of the dinosaurs, is extinct in the rest of the world.

Frilled lizard

To scare off predators, this lizard spreads out its neck frill, opens its mouth and hisses. If this doesn't work, then it will run away as fast as it can. Frilled lizards live in forests in northern Australia where they feed on termites, spiders and smaller lizards.

Saltwater crocodile

Averaging more than 5 m in length, the massive saltwater crocodile is the biggest and most dangerous crocodile in the world. A top predator, this crocodile can kill almost anything in its way, including large prey such as water buffalo. Fossil evidence suggests that this crocodile species could be 4 million years old.

Habitat Focus:
Great Barrier Reef

Extending for over 2,000 km, the Great Barrier Reef lies off the northeast coast of Australia. It is the largest coral reef on Earth. The warm, shallow waters of the reef teem with plant and animal life. Coral reefs contain about one quarter of the world's marine life, but they are under threat from global warming, over-fishing, pollution and tourism. Corals are slow-growing so, for this reason, many countries are now protecting corals.

Porcupine fish

This fish is sometimes called a 'puffer fish' because of the way it puffs its body up like a balloon in order scare its enemies. When it does this the spines on its scales stand on end and it is impossible to eat.

Coral

Corals may look like plants but, in fact, they are tiny animals. They have a mouth and stomach in the centre of their stem and a protective skeleton on the outside. There are hundreds of species of coral on the reef. Corals connect with each other to form colonies. The algae that live on the coral give it colour and food.

Clown anemone fish

Also called the 'clown fish', these fish live amongst the stinging tentacles of anemones. A chemical on the skin of the clown fish makes it immune from the sting of the anemone!

Parrot fish

The parrot fish has a beak-like mouth that it uses to bite off pieces of coral and plants. It also has an extra set of teeth at the back of its mouth that it uses to grind up its food into smaller pieces.

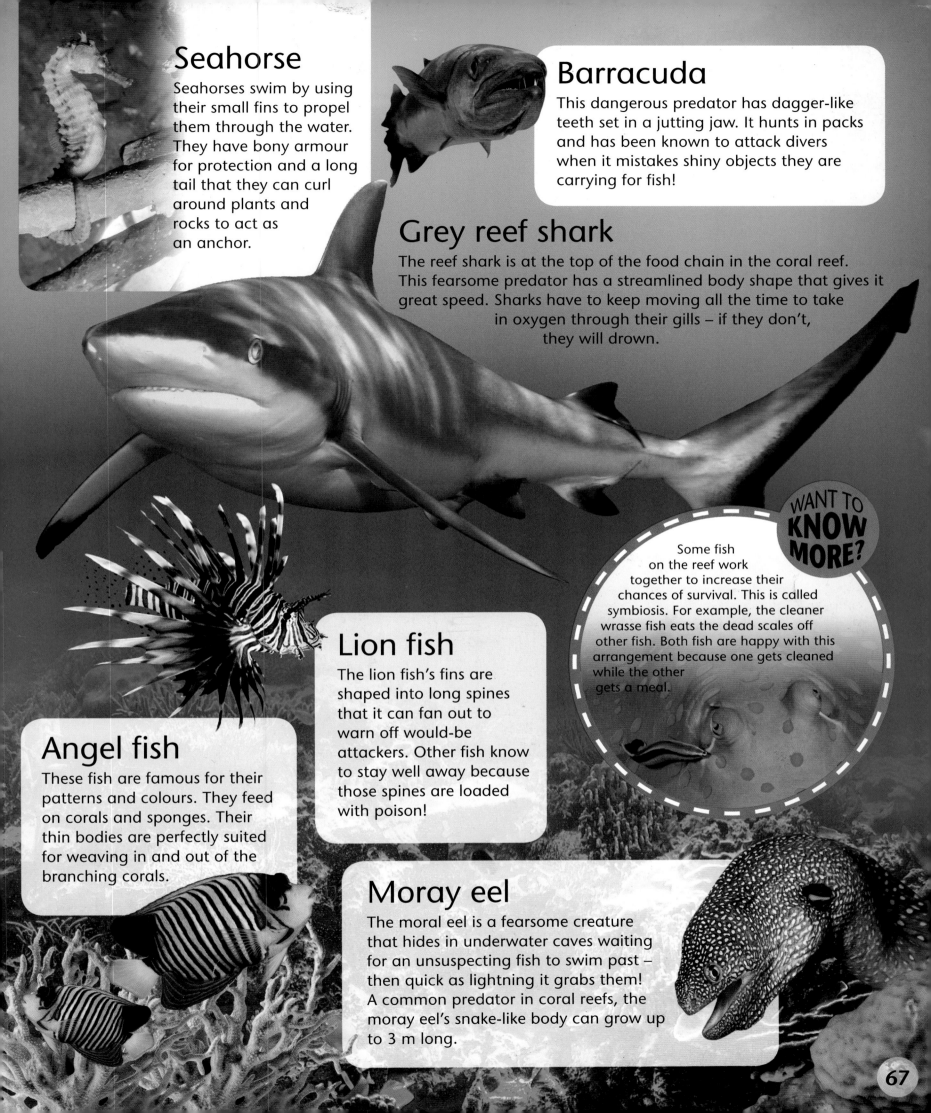

Seahorse

Seahorses swim by using their small fins to propel them through the water. They have bony armour for protection and a long tail that they can curl around plants and rocks to act as an anchor.

Barracuda

This dangerous predator has dagger-like teeth set in a jutting jaw. It hunts in packs and has been known to attack divers when it mistakes shiny objects they are carrying for fish!

Grey reef shark

The reef shark is at the top of the food chain in the coral reef. This fearsome predator has a streamlined body shape that gives it great speed. Sharks have to keep moving all the time to take in oxygen through their gills – if they don't, they will drown.

WANT TO KNOW MORE?

Some fish on the reef work together to increase their chances of survival. This is called symbiosis. For example, the cleaner wrasse fish eats the dead scales off other fish. Both fish are happy with this arrangement because one gets cleaned while the other gets a meal.

Lion fish

The lion fish's fins are shaped into long spines that it can fan out to warn off would-be attackers. Other fish know to stay well away because those spines are loaded with poison!

Angel fish

These fish are famous for their patterns and colours. They feed on corals and sponges. Their thin bodies are perfectly suited for weaving in and out of the branching corals.

Moray eel

The moral eel is a fearsome creature that hides in underwater caves waiting for an unsuspecting fish to swim past – then quick as lightning it grabs them! A common predator in coral reefs, the moray eel's snake-like body can grow up to 3 m long.

Antarctica

The frozen continent of Antarctica is surrounded by the Southern Ocean, and at its centre is the South Pole. People don't live here permanently because it is too cold, though scientists have set up research stations to monitor the environment. In winter, the ice on Antarctica can be up to 4 km thick. With temperatures falling as low as –80 °C, the animals that live here display amazing adaptations and extreme survival skills.

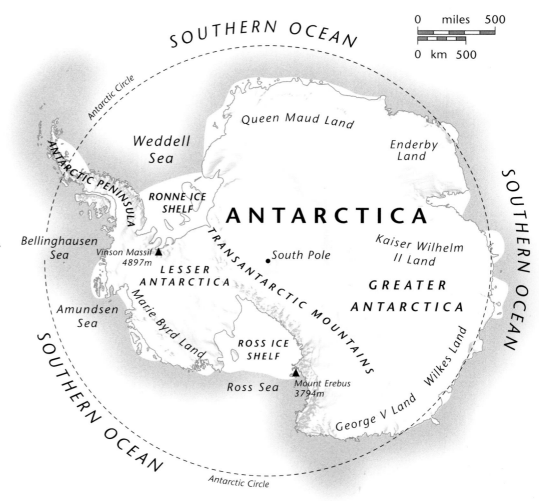

Krill

Looking similar to shrimps, krill are the crustaceans that are a vital link in the Antarctic food chain. Feeding on plankton, sea plants and small sea creatures, they are the main diet of whales, seals, fish, squid and birds – in fact, most marine animals eat krill.

Emperor penguin

Adapted to the worst weather on Earth, emperor penguins have layers of scale-like feathers and stores of fat to insulate their bodies and provide energy. They grip the ice with their claws when walking, or slide about on their tummies. In the water, their aerodynamic shape is perfect for swimming and diving. Their main predators are leopard seals and killer whales.

Blue whale

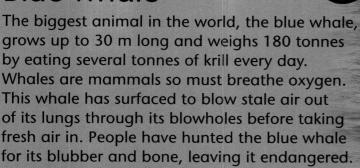

The biggest animal in the world, the blue whale, grows up to 30 m long and weighs 180 tonnes by eating several tonnes of krill every day. Whales are mammals so must breathe oxygen. This whale has surfaced to blow stale air out of its lungs through its blowholes before taking fresh air in. People have hunted the blue whale for its blubber and bone, leaving it endangered.

Squid

An important link in the Antarctic food chain, squid will eat almost anything. Their arms and tentacles grab whatever passes their way. In turn, they are prey for sharks and whales. Like octopus and cuttlefish, they move by propulsion – they squirt a jet of water to propel themselves in the opposite direction.

Albatross

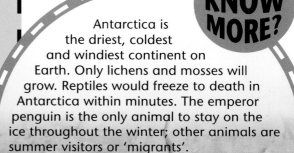

The albatross conserves energy by soaring on currents of air. Its large specialised wings are adapted for long-distance flying. For example, it has a shoulder-lock that locks the wings into place. Its nostrils run down the length of its beak so that it can smell prey (fish and squid) in the sea as it flies overhead.

WANT TO KNOW MORE?

Antarctica is the driest, coldest and windiest continent on Earth. Only lichens and mosses will grow. Reptiles would freeze to death in Antarctica within minutes. The emperor penguin is the only animal to stay on the ice throughout the winter; other animals are summer visitors or 'migrants'.

Antarctic icefish

The icefish has anti-freeze in its blood to stop it from freezing in the icy Antarctic waters. It has gills, but can also breathe directly through its skin. Its large eyes provide better vision in the dark waters beneath the ice.

Crabeater seal

Despite their name, these crabeater seals do not eat crabs – they prefer krill. Their pointed teeth are specially shaped for filtering krill from the water and their streamlined bodies are ideal for diving. In spring, they will breed and bring up their pups on the pack ice. When summer ends their skin becomes almost white as camouflage against the snow.

Glossary

Adaptation The process of changing to suit conditions in the environment

Amphibian Cold-blooded animals that breed in water, but as adults, spend time on land

Arachnid An animal with eight legs and a body divided into two segments

Arctic tundra Flat, treeless ground that is almost permanently frozen

Bioluminous A word that can describe an animal that has luminous body parts, e.g. the angler fish

Biome An area of the world that has a particular climate and range of plant life

Bird A warm-blooded animal that has a beak, wings, feathers and two legs

Camouflage A colour or pattern that an animal uses to blend into its environment

Carnivore An animal that eats other animals

Carrion The decaying body of a dead animal

Cephalopod A mollusc with a large head and tentacles, such as a squid

Climate The average weather recorded over a long period

Conservation Protection of habitats or living things in the environment

Consumer An animal in a food chain that eats (consumes) plants or other animals

Continent One of the Earth's seven largest land masses: Africa, Asia, Australia, Antarctica, Europe, North America, South America

Crustacean An animal that has a hard outer shell (exoskeleton) protecting its body, antennae and several pairs of legs

Deciduous A word that can describe a plant that sheds its leaves each year, e.g. sycamore and birch

Desert An area that has less than 25 cm of rainfall per year

Echo location When an animal such as a bat or dolphin makes a sound then listens to the returning echo to locate objects

Ecosystem Animals and plants that depend on each other in a particular habitat

Endangered A word that can describe an animal or plant species that is in danger of becoming extinct

Environment The surroundings or climate conditions in which a plant or animal lives

Evergreen A word that can describe a plant that keeps its leaves throughout the year, e.g. fir and pine

Evolution A favourable change of a species over time that can result in a new species

Exoskeleton A protective skeleton on the outside of the body such as on an insect

Extinct A word that can describe an animal or plant species that is no longer living and has died out completely

Fish A cold-blooded animal that lives in water, breathes through gills and has scales and fins

Food chain A chain of living things, each feeding on the other

Habitat A place where an animal lives, e.g. a forest or a desert

Herbivore An animal that eats only plants

Hibernation A long sleep that shuts down an animal's body, usually over winter

Insect An animal with six legs and a segmented body; it usually has wings

Invertebrate An animal without a backbone, e.g. a worm, snail or spider

Larva An early stage in the life cycle of butterflies, ants and other insects

Mammal A warm-blooded animal that produces milk to feed its young; it usually has fur or hair

Mangrove A tropical evergreen tree with roots that are exposed at low tide

Marsupial An animal with a pouch in which its young develop

Migration The journeys animals make to find seasonal food supplies

Molar A large, flat tooth used for crushing and chewing food

Mollusc An animal with a soft body that is usually protected by a shell

Monsoon A word that describes the rainy season or torrential rainfall

Omnivore An animal that eats plants and other animals

Plankton Microscopic plants and animals living near the surface of lakes and oceans

Prairie A flat, grass-covered plain in the USA or Canada

Predator An animal that kills other animals for food

Prey The animals that predators eat

Producer An organism that can produce its own food, e.g. a plant or algae

Reptile A cold-blooded animal that has scaly skin and lays eggs from which its young hatch

Savannah Flat grassland in the tropics or the subtropics

Scavenger An animal that does not hunt, but instead feeds on dead animals, or carrion

Species Animals or plants that share similar features and can produce offspring together

Symbiosis A close connection between different species of living things that has advantages for each species involved

Temperate A climate that is mild or without extremes of hot or cold is temperate

Territory An area that an animal or group of animals have claimed as their home

Tropical A tropical climate is very hot and humid throughout the year

Vertebrate An animal with a backbone, e.g. a fish, mammal, bird or reptile

Index of Animals

The Continents

NORTH
AMERICA

ATLANTIC
OCEAN

PACIFIC
OCEAN

SOUTH
AMERICA

SOUTHERN
OCEAN

ANTARCTICA